"I've been burned once really badly and I'm afraid of getting hustled into another disaster."

"I'm dating these two wonderful guys. . . . I'll never forgive myself if I choose the wrong one."

"My marriage is going to pieces and I can't seem to do anything about it."

LOVING SMART

When it comes to being in love, how does anyone make sensible, rational decisions? How can couples, in the heat of anger or passion, identify underlying problems? For the first time, here is real and effective help for anyone who needs to get past the complicated, often contradictory feelings and make rational, intelligent choices.

This book gives you 66 actual Smartcards to pull out, look at, and then sort into a specially devised system that will help you—or your partner—prioritize your relationship and get a better understanding of what you need to change. . . .

From **HANDLING MONEY** to **HAVING SEX**, from **BEING CONSID-ERATE** to **BEING ROMANTIC**, every Smartcard labels an aspect of your relationship. And by comparing your cards with the extensive case histories and probing questions raised in this book, you will get new insight into yourself, your partner, and what smart loving is really all about.

LOVING SMART

LOVING SMART

PUTTING YOUR CARDS ON THE TABLE

DR. JEFFREY TITLE
ELISE TITLE, M.S.W., AND JACQUELINE TITLE, M.A.

WARNER BOOKS

A Time Warner Company

Warner Books, Inc., 1271 Avenue of the Americas, New York, NY 10020

 A Time Warner Company

Printed in the United States of America
First printing: September 1993
10 9 8 7 6 5 4 3 2 1

Library of Congress Cataloging-in-Publication Data

Title, Jeffrey.
    Loving smart / Jeffrey Title, Elise Title, and Jacqueline Title.
      p.   cm.
    ISBN 0-446-39433-5
    1. Intimacy (Psychology)   2. Love.   3. Interpersonal relations.
I. Title, Elise, 1943– . II. Title, Jacqueline, 1936–
III. Title.
BF575.I5T58   1993
152.4'1—dc20   92-32441
                                       CIP

Cover design by Julia Kushnirsky
Cover illustration by Linda Bleck
Book design by Giorgetta Bell McRee

ATTENTION: SCHOOLS AND CORPORATIONS

WARNER books are available at quantity discounts with bulk purchase for educational, business, or sales promotional use. For information, please write to: SPECIAL SALES DEPARTMENT, WARNER BOOKS,1271 AVENUE OF THE AMERICAS, NEW YORK, N.Y. 10020.

ARE THERE WARNER BOOKS
YOU WANT BUT CANNOT FIND IN YOUR LOCAL STORES?

You can get any WARNER BOOKS title in print. Simply send title and retail price, plus 50¢ per order and 50¢ per copy to cover mailing and handling costs for each book desired. New York State and California residents add applicable sales tax. Enclose check or money order only, no cash please, to: WARNER BOOKS, P.O. BOX 690, NEW YORK, N.Y. 10019.

To Helen Rees
who was with us all the way

I was married once. It was the result of a misunderstanding between myself and the young woman.

Oscar Wilde
The Importance of Being Earnest

CONTENTS

ACKNOWLEDGMENTS

Jeff and Elise would like to acknowledge three very special and loving couples whose marriages are the envy of all who know them. They have been our loyal supporters throughout the years *Loving Smart* has been in the works, providing us with great ideas and boundless encouragement. Thanks to—Joanna Schwartz and Joe Schwartz, M.D. (Joe told us the jokes we used in the introduction to *Loving Smart*); Deanna Spielberg, Ed.D., and Ted Spielberg, M.D.; Marilyn Dawber, M.S.W., and Bill Dawber, M.S.W.

Jacqueline would like to thank her dear friends on both coasts who, with their personal honesty and integrity, have shared through the years their innermost concerns, deepest fears, and greatest hopes about life and relationships. By doing so, they have inspired many of the questions in this book.

LOVING SMART

INTRODUCTION

A middle-aged woman sits down beside a middle-aged man on a park bench and gives him a long, scrutinizing stare. The man turns to her.

"Why are you looking at me like that?" he asks.

"You look just like my third husband," she tells him.

"So, how many times have you been married?"

Her eyes twinkle. "Twice."

By poking fun at our foibles, jokes help us face painful realities. It's pretty scary to think how often we exercise little more judgment than the lady in the joke when it comes to picking a mate. The joke's funny because it's so close to the truth.

Yearning for love, wanting that wonderful, exhilarating feeling, that sense of connection, can lead us to abandon reason and common sense, and take us down the road of desperation. Take Becky, for example.

Becky meets Louie at a social club in Miami.

"So, how come I never saw you here before?" she asks.

"I live here, but I've been away for a while," he says.

"So, where were you?" she asks.

1

"I was in jail for twenty years," he tells her.

"So, what did you do that you were in jail for twenty years?" she asks.

"Well, I took an ax and I chopped my wife up into itsy bitsy pieces," he says.

She gives her newly permed silver hair a little pat and smiles up at the man.

"So," she drawls, "you're single."

Many of us want intimate love in our lives so badly that we blind ourselves to our partners' flaws. We get in too deep, too early, and fail to come to our senses until it's too late. Hopefully, not as late as it was for that parolee's ex-wife, but, sadly still, late enough to make divorce a likely solution to our problems.

Human nature can be humorously and horribly pernicious. Sometimes it seems like half the world is going to any length to secure a mate, while the lucky half who have them are devoted to squandering their blessings. Take Max for example—please.

For thirty years, Sophie has demanded two dollars from her husband, Max, every time they've made love. Now on their thirtieth anniversary, they're celebrating in Florida.

"Sophie, tell me," Max says. "What did you do with all those dollars you've collected over the years?"

"Look out the window, Max. What do you see?"

"I see a motel, a restaurant, a swimming pool . . ."

"Max," Sophie says tenderly, "everything you see is yours. I took all those dollars from all those years and invested them so you'd have a nice nest egg for your old age."

Max starts to shake his head and cry.

"Max, what's the matter?" Sophie asks anxiously.

Max gives his loving wife a teary-eyed look.

"Sophie, Sophie, if only I would have known you were such a good investor," he cries, "I would have given you *all* of my business!"

Do you know a good thing when you have it? Or a lousy thing for that matter? Do you see love as a strictly hit-or-miss affair? Do you always end up thinking that the person you don't have is more desirable than the one you do have? Have you already thrown up your hands in disgust, after one or more disappointments, heartaches, or failures? Do you question why a relationship isn't working or never worked? Do you know what went wrong? Do you know what went right? Do you keep making the same mistakes?

Awareness and intentional behavior are the keys to mastering intimacy and creating lasting love relationships. You need a relatively dispassionate approach to a totally passionate situation, using your full intelligence and thoughtful control of your behavior to succeed.

Jim's Approach

For more than twenty-five years in my counseling practice, I've been supporting a carefully considered, Loving Smart approach to intimacy with couples and individuals, and I've been practicing what I preach in my marriage. I've combined instruction in how to adopt the most effective attitudes, ideas, and behaviors that make intimacy work, and warnings to avoid those that lead to failure. One of my primary goals has been to demystify romance and "that funny thing called love."

Sometimes I've felt up against it, preaching my Loving Smart approach in a culture that's so wrapped up in a romantic view of love. "But Dr. Title, if you've got to think too much about what you're doing," various patients have protested, "it spoils everything." Right. And ruining your life with a succession of heartbreaking, failed relationships is a better alternative? After witnessing so much unhappiness in the individuals and couples I've treated, I feel passionate about getting the message out that Loving Smart is a huge improvement over letting your mindless hormones rule your love life and ultimately lead you to despair.

In the past, it took weeks and sometimes months to untangle the vast complexities and muddled, chaotic emotions tied up in my patients' intimate relationships. The process was more than a bit arduous, and with relationships being so multilayered and elaborate, we were inevitably backtracking later on, filling in issues we'd skipped over.

When I introduced the Smartcards to my practice, the process of nailing down that all-important comprehensive picture of the relationship in question got an immeasurable boost. The Smartcards, developed by me and my coauthors, were really quite revolutionary for the people who first tried them out. I've been using them in my practice for eight years, and the benefit to my patients has been considerable. Instead of endless hours of protracted, drawn-out, and often insufficient discussion of what was going on in a relationship, patients could simply "put their cards on the table." The good, the bad, and the ugly—all of the issues, positive and negative, laid out, right before our eyes. The effect was electric, the task brisk, engrossing, satisfying, and fun.

The creation of the Smartcards began with my sister and coauthor Jackie, a speech therapist who is single. She had developed an extensive list of relationship factors and questions that she felt needed to be asked when dating or choosing a prospective partner. She thought that anyone who was dating could benefit from this approach. As she put it, "it's always better to have too much information than too little, even if it hurts." When she tried out the questions with her friends, they thought it was great fun and raised their awareness of similarities and differences between themselves and their partners.

Jackie showed her checklist to my wife Elise, and me. We loved the idea. It coincided perfectly with my theories, practice, and philosophy. I wanted to develop it further to use with my psychology patients in all stages of their intimate relationships. Elise, a clinical social worker for fifteen years, who'd recently turned romance novelist, was full of ideas about the big relationship picture.

In the end, we combined Jackie's years of dating experience with our decades of happy marriage and clinical experience to developed an exhaustive set of relationship issues. After much brainstorming, we came up with the notion of putting the issues on cards, which we dubbed Smartcards, so they could be readily grouped and compared. I then created a sorting and ranking system for the Smartcards which allowed my patients to gain an in-depth perspective of the many factors at play in their relationships, allowing them to evaluate the issues more openly and honestly.

The discoveries, insights, and changes so many of my patients made as a result of using the Smartcards would warm the cockles of any psychotherapist's heart. They certainly did mine. And since that time, I've been refining, redefining, and expanding the Smartcards themselves and the methods for using them to sort out intimate relationships.

The Loving Smart program we're presenting here combines the Smartcards process with the theories and methods of intentional, clear-headed loving I've been developing and using with patients throughout my career. The program is designed to give you control of your love life.

Loving Smart means learning how to put your head where your heart has customarily been. In Part One of *Loving Smart,* we teach you how to put your cards on the table, literally and figuratively. We give you the tools for doing this with our unique Smartcard sort, a hands-on, easy-to-follow method for acquiring a realistic, unsentimental view of what's happening in your relationship. To get further clarification on the issues when you begin your Smartcard sort, you can refer to Chapter Five, which contains thought-provoking questions for each card. These questions can help you get a better feel for any card if you're unsure of how to interpret it, or where it should be placed. Once your cards are on the table, you will record your results on the worksheets we've included so that you can take note of any changes that occur over time, or make comparisons between different intimate relationships.

Next, we show you how to examine and evaluate your Smartcard sort so that you can determine for yourself whether your relationship is viable and, if it is, precisely what issues need to be addressed to make it better. Here, you will turn again to the questions section we provide in Chapter Five. By answering the questions for the cards you have put on the table, you will be able to explore the layers of meaning each of the issues has for you. We'll also teach you a wide variety of ways to use the Smartcards to stay smart in your ongoing relationship, or to start out on the right foot with someone new.

In Part Two of *Loving Smart,* you'll gain the essential knowledge base of the practical psychology and philosophy of successful, enduring love. I warn you away from the dangerous myths of romantic love, and the irrational fears and unproductive thought patterns that block intimacy. You'll learn the architecture of good love relationships so that you can build the kind of solid foundation necessary to weather the vicissitudes of long-term loving. Lastly, I share the most essential behaviors and attitudes that you need to start off on the right foot in a relationship and learn how to keep your love on the right track—unlike Jennifer and Nick.

> Jennifer and Nick meet at an upscale Manhattan singles' bar. Nick saunters up to Jennifer, they chat for a couple of minutes, then she gives him a come-hither smile and murmurs, "Your place or mine?"
>
> "Hey," Nick says, backing off, "if it's gonna be a hassle, forget it."

We think the "hassle" is more than worth it. Once you've got the Loving Smart program down pat, you have the best chance for ending up with the love of your life and the last laugh.

PART ONE

PUTTING YOUR CARDS ON THE TABLE

CHAPTER ONE

THE LOVING SMART PROGRAM

THE SMARTCARDS IN ACTION

On an unusually sunny March day, Joan comes to my office for the first time. A vibrant, bright, attractive thirty-six-year-old college professor, Joan makes it clear even before she sits down that she's not interested in long-term psychotherapy. She is leaving on a sabbatical in five weeks and she wants to deal with this pressing problem in the time she has left.

Joan prides herself on being very open, insightful, and psychologically savvy. She says right out that she is the typical child of very demanding parents—something of a worrier and a perfectionist, and could easily become a workaholic. But that is not her reason for making an appointment. She has come to talk about the man she is dating. In her efficient style she fills in the background. She's been married and divorced twice, and is now involved with an extremely brilliant and dynamic lawyer with whom she's madly in love. I hear the passion in her voice as she tells me William is everything she's been looking for in a man—he is good-looking, urbane, incredibly successful, charming, attentive, a terrific lover, and single.

I smile at her. "So what's the problem?"

Joan gives me an earnest look and with absolute sincerity replies, "Something's missing."

There is a dramatic change in Joan's demeanor. This assertive,

9

high-powered woman abruptly slumps back in her seat, tears springing to her eyes. She quickly apologizes, telling me her friends accuse her of simply never being satisfied with a man. It seems that way to her at times too.

I ask Joan if she can pinpoint what's missing in the relationship, but she merely shrugs, saying it's more a gut feeling. The uncharacteristic vagueness of her response reveals tremendous inner turmoil. Does she have *any* ideas about the source of the problem? Not really, she replies, although she's fretted about it a great deal. After all, she tells me, she's a two-time loser in the intimacy game and she dreads the thought of failing again.

In a flood of words, she reveals that she feels very guilty about the failure of her two marriages, although, even as we sit together in my office, she can't really put her finger on what went wrong in either case. She thinks maybe she was too young when she married her first husband, but she doesn't think she was really very immature. As for her second marriage, for a long time she attributed the breakup to her husband's unwillingness to compromise and to a general feeling of incompatibility, but now she feels that somehow—she doesn't know how—she had more to do with the problem.

I have no doubt that Joan is a discerning, articulate woman who is in control of many aspects of her life. However, when it comes to highly charged intimate relationships, Joan, like many people, loses her mooring. Much of what goes on between her and the men she cares about is, for her, shrouded in mystery. I press the issue and she admits to often feeling overwhelmed and confused, allowing her emotions to guide her even when she isn't all that clear about what she is feeling. In short, she confesses that when she is in love, a feeling she cherishes, ironically she also feels quite powerless.

I bring Joan back to her original problem. "You say something is missing in your relationship with William. Would you like to sort out what's missing?"

"Absolutely," Joan says, adding again that she is not looking for a long-term analysis.

I smile, withdraw a deck of Smartcards from my top drawer, and say, "How about sorting it all out right now? How about putting your cards on the table?"

I extend the deck of Smartcards to her and she gives me a wary, questioning look. It is a look I've grown familiar with over the past eight years.

"Look through the cards. Just give them each a glance," I encourage. "There are sixty-six Smartcards with a different issue heading on each, representing one aspect of an intimate relationship."

Joan cautiously takes hold of the Smartcard deck. As soon as she starts going through them, the caution fades as another dramatic change transforms her demeanor, every bit as typical to me as her initial wariness. I watch her as she pauses and smiles at some cards, even chuckles at a few, frowns and shakes her head at others. Her body relaxes into the chair and she takes a firmer grip on the cards. She looks intrigued, attentive, alert without the aggressive edge.

"Okay," I tell her, tapping the desk in front of her, "now I want you to sort the Smartcards out into four stacks—one, for those issues that you see as positive features in your relationship, those areas where the two of you are compatible; two, for those issues you see as negatives in your relationship, meaning those areas where the two of you are having problems, arguments, or concerns . . ."

At this point Joan cuts me off. "We really don't have any negatives."

"If there are any cards that might be trouble spots or disappointments you can add them to that stack," I tell her. "In the third stack, I want you to put down cards that are unknowns. Issues that you'd like to know more about. Set the leftover cards aside in a discard stack, for the ones that don't seem to have any bearing."

Joan goes through the Smartcards again, this time with more active involvement. After a while she comments that she never realized how many issues were at play in a relationship. In her first run-through it is very easy for Joan to put down the cards for the positive stack: **EXPRESSING LOVE, BEING RELIABLE, HAVING A SENSE OF HUMOR, POLITICAL VIEWS, HAVING FUN,** and more.

Joan is very upbeat when she looks at this stack. "We really do have a lot going for us," she remarks, buoyed.

Without coaxing, she returns to the remaining Smartcards, this second run-through more thoughtful and penetrating. She selects each card, holds it out, examines it, considers it. Much to her surprise she places a great number of the remaining cards on her stack of unknowns. She finds this very perplexing.

"I thought I knew everything I ever wanted to know about William without really trying," she jokes, but there's a serious look in her eyes.

Little by little, Joan begins considering Smartcards for her negative stack. Finally, as she places one down, I can see, and she reports feeling, a physical strain. She admits that **MOOD AND EMOTIONAL ISSUES** is somewhat problematic. William is very cool under fire and, while he doesn't belittle her when she feels anxious or upset after a particularly stressful department meeting, he does seem to distance himself more from her at those times. Equally, Joan finds William's even temper frustrating and intimidating at times. And whereas she'd never before viewed herself as a particularly moody person, now, because of William's flat responsiveness, she worries that maybe she is too moody.

Once Joan places that first card in the negative stack, she gains confidence about looking at other negatives. She realizes that she isn't making judgments so much as examining, for the first time, the more subtle and complex factors at play between her and William. She isn't looking at what is wrong with William or with herself, but rather is considering what issues cause her concern within the relationship. For example, there is nothing intrinsically negative about William being even-tempered. In itself, Joan considers it an especially fine trait. It's how his mood meshes or doesn't mesh with her mood at varying times, and how these contrasts play themselves out within the relationship, that troubles her.

When Joan finishes putting her cards on the table, she has a half-dozen in the negative stack. But she's not feeling down about all those negatives. Instead, she feels buoyed by her discovery that those nebulous, uncomfortable feelings she's been experiencing are due, in part, to a few particular sticking points, and mostly to so many unexplored issues.

Next, when I have Joan rank her Smartcards from the most significant to the least significant issue in each stack, she's surprised to find that she has no trouble ordering her negative stack. Now that she can see the items and consider what they mean to her, she knows immediately what weight to give each. On top of her negative list is **SHOWING OPENNESS**. This is a significantly troubling issue, she realizes now. Joan likes to say what is on her mind. She doesn't want to hold back. She doesn't want secrets that would lead to suspicions. William, she acknowledges now, isn't very open. He doesn't like talking about himself and often makes jokes about not wanting to spoil the mystery when she presses him at all.

As Joan talks about the other negatives in her stack, lifting each of them up in turn, tapping them, holding them out, she's amazed to find she can look at these issues with so much objectivity and perception. Best of all, she's not feeling any guilt or assigning any blame.

Looking at her ordered stacks of Smartcards at the end of the session, Joan says she feels a new sense of mastery. Sorting out what is going on with William is no longer a vague cerebral process. She now has an active, hands-on tool to figure out and evaluate her relationship as well as past relationships and potential future ones. She can take the Smartcards with her and use them at her leisure.

The most exciting part for Joan is finding a mechanism for solving the mystery of what is "missing" with William. Now, instead of uneasy feelings that provoke anxiety, she has tangible issues of concern to focus on. She can name the problems, evaluate how important they are to her, and decide what she wants to do about them. Joan resolves to discuss these issues with William. What helps to encourage her is seeing the problems in the context of the many positives within their relationship. Instead of merely zeroing in on negatives she can also talk to William about all they have going for them. Joan feels confident that doing the Smartcards not only is proving insightful to her, but will open up meaningful areas of communication between her and William.

Taking hold of the cards in her unknown stack, Joan ponders them, aware that by filling in the gaps she will get more of a sense of where her relationship might go, how it might develop, even what stumbling blocks might come up along the way. Most significantly, she can begin to think about these issues now and take an active hand in dealing with them as her relationship with William progresses.

Joan is finding the process of using the Smartcards to sort out her relationship increasingly exhilarating. She can't wait to do the Smartcards for her past marriages to see what else she can learn. "Just how much does history repeat itself?" she wonders. Then she picks up her deck of Smartcards and says, "Not this time."

As Joan indicated to me when she triumphantly raised the cards in her fist, the Smartcard sort imparts a sense of power and control over one of life's most emotionally runaway problems.

Joan is typical of countless people struggling to untangle the mystery and complexity of their intimate relationships. Before she used the Smartcards, exploring her relationships was a matter of endless ruminating, often fruitless or even destructive conversations with her boyfriends, and, as her last resort, a visit to the psychologist. Without the help of the Smartcards, her intimacy problems were simply too complex and elusive for her to identify, much less keep straight in her mind. With the Smartcards in hand, the process of making sense out of her romantic involvement was an engaging, uplifting experience.

During our subsequent counseling sessions I helped Joan expand the understanding she gained from her initial sorting of the Smartcards. The additional steps were designed to allow her to delve more deeply into the most positive and negative aspects of her relationship with William and then put it all in the context of the broader philosophic and psychological underpinnings of achieving a successful relationship.

THE MAGIC OF THE SMARTCARDS

Like Joan, dozens of women and men I've seen in my practice have found something almost magically invigorating and empowering about using the Smartcards to explore relationships. The magic is in the Smartcards themselves.

Taking the Smartcard deck in hand—literally taking hold of the issues in your relationship—provides you with an immediate sense of control. With that sense of control comes a lifting of your spirits. You have moved from a passive to an active approach to your life. The simple process of taking up a card representing an emotion-laden issue creates the second bit of magic. Holding up the card provides just enough distance to free you to look at the issue and examine your concerns. Emotionally charged issues are dealt with by your brain in ways that are designed to keep you from becoming too upset. Often, the mere thought of an issue steeped in inner conflict causes a full-fledged mental retreat. This is an area where your healthy brain's attempt to keep you feeling okay has the unfortunate side effect of preventing you from contemplating your problem, and, therefore, keeps you from doing anything about it.

Looking at an issue on a Smartcard gives your brain the idea that the issue itself is outside you—as it resides on an innocuous card. This little bit of distancing is often just enough to give the part of you that wants to deal with your problems a chance to override the part that wants to protect you from hurt. It's a small mental twist with a powerful effect. This is the kind of magic that unlocks the doors to very complex feelings and lets you begin to master your love life.

CHAPTER TWO

WHO CAN BENEFIT FROM USING THE SMARTCARDS?

Here are some examples of people who have benefited from putting their Smartcards on the table, to give you a feel for when you can use the Smartcards and what you're likely to learn. They will demonstrate that the answer to the question "Who can benefit from using the Smartcards?" is everyone in an intimate relationship or wishing to be, as well as everyone struggling to understand what went wrong after a breakup.

WHEN YOU'VE JUST BEGUN TO DATE SOMEONE

"I've dated this guy a few times and I can't decide if the relationship has any real potential. Am I wasting my time? Is this relationship right for me?"

Karen, a thirty-seven-year-old single woman, thinks Pete's a nice guy but "he's completely different from the type of man I usually go out with." Karen is a lawyer and she describes her usual date as a

15

"professional" man. On the other hand, Pete, a brash, burly man in his mid-forties, is a contractor with a high school education. They met while he was doing a small renovation on her kitchen.

When Pete first asked her out, Karen was hesitant. However, she admits she found Pete "refreshingly uncomplicated" and "incredibly sexy." She accepted the date, telling herself it would be "a novelty, a one-shot deal."

On their first date, Pete suggested bowling. Karen reluctantly agreed, only to discover she had a lot of fun. Enough fun to accept two more dates with Pete—a movie and pizza one night, and a local rock concert another. She had a great time on both dates, but while Karen clearly enjoyed spending time with Pete, she is concerned that Pete doesn't really fit into her life. While she believes it's too soon to consider whether Pete is marriage material, she is very conscious of not wanting to get involved in a relationship at this point in her life that isn't likely to develop into something with serious "potential."

Karen says her chief concern is the difference in their professional status, but when she does the Smartcard sort, although that comes up as an issue of concern, several others take precedence. Topping her stack of negative Smartcards is the value and role of **HOBBIES AND OUTSIDE INTERESTS.** Karen is a little taken aback by how highly she rates this issue. Her first reaction to the card was that it was a silly issue for us to have included in the Smartcard set. In the sorting process, however, the card focused her attention on a troubling difference between her and Pete. In their few dates she learned that he's a man who always fills his time with activities. When he's not working, he bowls, plays on a softball team, rides his snowmobile, follows football and baseball on TV. Karen, on the other hand, finds her work as a lawyer so draining that she prefers quiet relaxation and getting together with friends for dinner and conversation in the spare time she ekes out for herself. Several other negatives she selects are **ETHNIC/CULTURAL/ SOCIAL/SPIRITUAL/RELIGIOUS VALUES, ISSUES OF TASTE, SET- TING GOALS, POLITICAL VIEWS,** and **HABITS.** While all of these negatives are of some concern to Karen, she sees none of them as seriously troubling, especially when weighed against the positives.

Karen selects several strong positives—**HAVING FUN, BEING CO- OPERATIVE AND SHARING, BEING ROMANTIC, BEING POLITE, SHOWING OPENNESS,** and, topping her list, **LISTENING.** These prove to be very important and meaningful issues for Karen and more than balance out the negatives. She loves the fact that Pete not only "hears" but "listens" to her. And she finds that his openness encourages a deeper "listening" on her part as well. Reflecting on this insight she realizes that in many of her previous relationships there was so much competition just beneath the surface that listening often didn't take place on either side. Karen also finds Pete's "courtly" manners refreshing. Without being macho, he manages to be attentive and show respect, and he enjoys making her feel special. Karen confesses she enjoys it too.

However, the most important message Karen gets from putting her cards on the table isn't the insight into the positives or negatives in her relationship with Pete, but the number of unknowns that she stacks up. In a new relationship, this stack is often large—which surprises some people who are sure that after only a few dates they have a real feel for their new partner.

Karen is able to examine this stack and pull out the issues that she feels are vital for her to know more about before she can honestly predict whether this relationship has a shot. Weighing the positives and negatives thus far, she feels it's worth her effort to explore these issues. What she finds most enlightening is that the issue she thought weighed the most—the difference in their professional status—is not nearly as important as she thought it was. Had she not done the Smartcards, Karen believes that based on that one issue alone she would have very likely stopped dating Pete.

♥

> "I really think this new guy, Lloyd, is gonna work out, even though a few years back I probably would never have accepted a date with a man like him."

For some people at the early stages of a relationship, the Smartcard sort lays out enough problem areas to convince them, right off the bat, that they're wasting their time.

For the past month, Penny, a divorced forty-seven-year-old editor at a literary magazine and an ardent ballet buff, has been dating Lloyd, an artist who lives in her building. It's been a long time between dates for Penny and she is clearly invested in wanting this relationship with Lloyd to develop, even though she's not too happy that he's "a bit of an over-the-hill hippie type." Initially, she is very effusive about Lloyd's fine qualities—the one she highlights the most being a shared love of ballet—but there's an undercurrent of edginess in her manner. She becomes aware of it herself and explains that "Lloyd isn't much of a talker," but she quickly counters this with, "It gives him a mysterious, romantic air." She hurriedly goes on to talk about several other *positives.* Lloyd is dedicated to his work, very affectionate, uninhibited, and "isn't hung up on younger women."

I suggest to Penny that she first go through the Smartcards and select the ones that would be most important and meaningful to her in an *ideal* relationship. She has no trouble doing this, although she'd never thought much in the past about the type of intimate relationship she'd like to have with a man. After then doing the Smartcard sort about her relationship with Lloyd, Penny confronts the reality that almost all of the issues and values placed highest in her ideal sort are negatives in their relationship. She can see laid out on the table before her a compendium of issues of concern and conflicting views, and a lack in areas of utmost importance to her. Putting her cards on the table has forced her to acknowledge that her relationship with Lloyd is not going anywhere and she doesn't want it to go anywhere.

♥

> "I'm madly in love with Brian, but my friends keep telling
> me I'm making a big mistake."

Meg admits that she falls in love easily and that her infatuations often blind her to the realities of intimacy. This "blindness" is powered by her need to have everything in her love life be perfect. In traditional counseling there would have to be a long period of evaluation, discussion, and clarification before she gained much in the way of insight. The Smartcards speed up the process by presenting all the issues at once in a format that gives Meg enough distance to be objective.

Meg no sooner takes hold of the deck than she begins telling me how many people misunderstand Brian. "Maybe they find him difficult," she says, "but they don't really understand him!"

It isn't until Meg starts laying out her cards and seeing how many accumulate in the negative and unknown stacks that she's first able to step back from her infatuation and look at the relationship for what it is. She is shaken to see how many of the elements she values in a good relationship are missing with Brian despite her strong infatuation.

Two key Smartcards in her negative stack are **BEING RELIABLE** and **BEING SUPPORTIVE.** Brian is very unreliable, telling her he'll call on a certain day and then not phoning, always showing up late to pick her up, promising to help with a project and leaving her flat. Meg tells me that she's insecure and needs someone who can be supportive when she's upset. But Brian couldn't care less. When she's tried to talk to him about a personal problem or a crisis at work, he either brushes her off or accuses her of being petty or childish, or both. His idea of being supportive is to advise her to stand up on her own two feet. But, Meg says, "Maybe he's right, he's just helping me to conquer my problem."

In refining the negative stack with Meg I ask her to separate out any issues that are especially worrisome—the kind that are hard to forgive, even impossible to live with. Meg admits that **BEING HONEST, TRUSTING, BEING RELIABLE,** and **BEING SUPPORTIVE** are crucially important to her. After confronting herself with the truth about her relationship with Brian, Meg feels quite saddened, and wonders what comes next. One thing for sure, she's really seeing what's lacking in the relationship. Meg is no longer allowing herself to be blinded by her romantic infatuation. She'll have her eyes open, knowing what she has to work on if she chooses to continue the relationship.

♥

"He's such a great guy, but I just don't feel that wild physical rush with Tom."

Sometimes, falling in *like* is a better beginning than falling in *love*. Gina, a very attractive music critic, has been dating Tom, a man she describes as being "an all-around nice guy" but not as physically attractive or smooth as the men she's used to dating. She says she's "ashamed to admit it, but looks have always been very important to me." She's considering breaking off the relationship because she isn't "wildly in love." Her friends tell her she's crazy, that Tom is a great catch even if he isn't an Adonis.

While Gina can say very offhandedly that Tom's a "terrific guy," it's only after doing the Smartcard sort that she actually appreciates just how terrific he is and how well their needs, desires, and interests mesh. "We really have a wonderful relationship," she remarks with more than a little amazement in her voice. Gina thinks back on some of the men she's been involved with in the past whom she thought were physically very handsome and sexy. "If I compare them based on the good stuff the cards pointed out, none of those guys stacks up against Tom," she says with a bright smile on her face.

Having put her Smartcards on the table, Gina surveys them and comments that she would envy anyone in a relationship like this and can't believe she's lucky enough to be the one who's in it. Nor can she believe she almost let it slip through her fingers. It's clear to her that the

HAVING SEX and BEING ROMANTIC Smartcards are in her negative stack because she has made so little effort in those areas. She even remarks that she half expects that seeing all these wonderful aspects of her relationship with Tom will make her feel a stronger physical attraction to him.

Putting her Smartcards on the table awakened Gina to the real substance and potential in a relationship she might have abandoned too soon because the sexual attraction hadn't developed yet. For her the realization was enough to inspire loving feelings and encourage her openness to the development of more intimacy.

♥

"I've been burned once really badly and I'm afraid of getting hustled into another disaster."

Barry, an attractive forty-two-year-old computer analyst, comes to his session in a quandary. Recently divorced, he has begun dating a woman whom he finds very appealing and attractive. They met through a mutual friend and have gone out on several very enjoyable dates. And yet he's reluctant to call Ellen for another date. Things, he feels, are moving way too fast. He doesn't want to get involved again so soon after his divorce from Micky.

I push Barry to open up and discuss the specific fears and concerns he has about being seduced into something he isn't ready for. He responds with some vague generalities, falls into silence, sighs, gives me an unusually anxious look, and hesitantly tells me "it's really something else altogether."

The actual problem, he admits, is that "She reminds me of Micky. They have the same build, the same hair color. They even wear the same perfume." In rapid order, Barry goes on to list several other similarities between his ex-wife and Ellen that he finds unnerving. They're both involved in writing—Micky being a free-lance editor and Ellen's current job being a contributing writer to a computer magazine. They both love opera and classical music. They have similar taste in clothes and decorating. And politically, they could be twins.

Barry is terrified that, if he continues seeing Ellen, he will just be repeating the sins of the past. I take out the Smartcards and hand them to him. "Okay, let's see if that's true."

Twenty minutes later he's quite relieved. After sorting out the Smartcards that define his relationship with Ellen—the positives, the negatives, and the unknowns—he's stunned to discover how different his relationship with Ellen is. In a comforting number of areas he hadn't even considered, things are nothing like they were with his wife: BEING AFFECTIONATE, ATTITUDE TOWARD AGE AND AGING, DECISION MAKING, ISSUES IN HAVING OR RAISING CHILDREN, CARING FOR/ABOUT PETS AND PLANTS, HANDLING MONEY.

Of course, he's only known Ellen for a short time and he was married to Micky for more than twelve years, so I have him do another sorting out of the Smartcards based on his relationship with his ex-wife when they were first dating. Not only do the differences in the two relationships hold up, but Barry also sees that the seeds of his eventual breakup were present from the start with his ex. Barry is not repeating his past. Indeed, his parting comment to me is that if he'd done the Smartcards after he and Micky had been dating for a few months, it's quite possible that he might never have married her. At least, he would have made an effort to work out some problems right from the start.

♥

WHEN YOU'RE DATING MORE THAN ONE MAN

"I'm dating these two wonderful guys. I feel pressure to choose before I lose them both. I'll never forgive myself if I choose the wrong one."

Lenore, a secretary, is dating both an older, divorced physician and a younger man whom she describes as a radical activist who works in a drug treatment program. The physician, Fred, is pressing Lenore to enter a monogamous relationship. He tells her that while he isn't ready yet to marry again, he thinks their relationship is heading that way. Michael, the drug therapist, is content to have a more freewheeling relationship with Lenore, but he makes it clear to her that she is very special in his life and very important to him.

Lenore is attracted to both men, but for very different reasons. Her gut instinct tells her that Fred is the better catch and she should give up Michael, even though she feels a certain excitement and energy with Michael that isn't there for her with Fred.

Lenore does the Smartcards for her relationships with both Michael and Fred. The outcome is not what she expected at all. Her relationships with both men are more similar than she'd ever have guessed. She sees that, for both men, she's chosen the very same negatives for some issues that are absolutely vital to her. Most significantly, the top negative for both is ISSUES IN HAVING OR RAISING CHILDREN, but for different reasons. Fred has two grown children and doesn't want to start a new family. And Michael, who has never been married and has no children, has strong feelings against bringing children into such a "decomposing environment."

By the time Lenore finishes putting her Smartcards on the table, she is confident about not making more of a commitment to Fred just yet. She has a clear idea of what work she has to do in each relationship before she gets more deeply involved with either of them.

♥

WHEN YOU'RE HAVING TROUBLE GETTING INTO RELATIONSHIPS

"I do my share of dating, but I'm not impressed. Either they're unfulfilling, unsatisfactory, or disappointing, or all of the above."

Caroline, a twenty-eight-year-old travel agent, describes herself as having an acute, finely tuned nose for men, and after one or two dates, she can tell whether they're "worth the bother." Almost invariably, they're not. Although Caroline claims her instincts rarely fail her, family members and friends frequently accuse her of being too fussy, too much of a perfectionist. Her best friend, married with two children, tells Caroline that the truth is she's scared to death of intimacy and won't give any guy a chance to get too close.

Caroline decides to use the Smartcard sort to examine her most recent date, George, a man she met at a party. She went out with George three times, a point she emphasizes in order to prove that she does give a guy a chance. But as she puts it, "three strikes and he's out."

After Caroline does the Smartcard sort on her brief relationship with George, several insights come to light. Most significant is Caroline's discovery that George has more fine qualities than she had been willing to consider. While they were dating, she'd only thought about the negatives, focusing on qualities she found lacking in the relationship.

Now that she has stepped back from the experience and actually put her hands on a wide enough range of issues, she sees that there were more pluses than she'd imagined. Caroline also finds herself intrigued with the large stack of unknowns, admitting for the first time that maybe she was too quick to call the batter out.

She does a Smartcard sort for two other recent relationships, and these heighten her realization that she approaches most dates with a negative attitude. She's been so busy looking for her dates to slip up that she couldn't notice their positive qualities. Her narrow view, she acknowledges, keeps her from exploring the issues that would let her learn about the potential in a relationship. After she finishes her Smartcard sorts, she decides to give George a call.

♥

"I'm getting a reputation at school as a love-'em-and-leave-'em kind of guy. Now, this new girl that I'm really nuts about says she can't trust me."

Seth is a twenty-year-old college student, a well-built athletic young man with a quick smile and an appealing manner. He says that he came into his own in college, rarely having dated in high school because he felt very shy around girls and was self-conscious about a mild acne condition that then cleared up midway into his freshman year of college. "Girls started noticing me—pretty ones—and I was blown away." Seth fell in love with the first girl he dated that year. But after a few weeks, he started comparing her with all the other "great-looking girls on campus who would come on to me." Now in his junior year, Seth has had a long string of very short relationships. Regardless of his reputation as a womanizer—or maybe because of it—he has no trouble getting girlfriends. "I just can't seem to stick with any of them for too long."

Seth talks about his parents' fairly recent divorce and his mother's subsequent remarriage that isn't going well. He sees his dad with a new woman practically every time he visits him for school breaks. Is he following in his father's footsteps? Seth has begun dating Leslie, a young woman who he says is "really special." He adds, "I'd really like to make this relationship last. But Leslie insists I'm never gonna stick it out, and maybe she's right."

Putting his Smartcards on the table, Seth is disturbed to note that he really has no clue what a relationship is all about. Almost every card lands in the unknown stack or the discard stack. The few positives he selects are, not surprisingly, **BEING ROMANTIC, PERSONAL APPEAR-ANCE, USING BIRTH CONTROL, HAVING FUN, and HAVING SEX.** In his negative stack he puts **ATTITUDE TOWARD PAST RELATIONSHIPS** and **MAKING A COMMITMENT TO THE RELATIONSHIP.**

When Seth reflects back on other relationships with women, he comments that his Smartcard sorts would have been remarkably similar. Seeing all the relationship issues to which he's never given a moment's thought, Seth knows that at least he has lots of room for improvement. In the following weeks we spend most of our time together reviewing his discards, where we find the issues he needs to understand in order to create a relationship that has real substance.

Seth takes several decks of the Smartcards back with him to college, wanting not only his new girlfriend to use them, but also some of his friends who "are just as naive as I am about what a relationship is all about."

♥

WHEN YOU'RE INVOLVED IN A LONG-TERM RELATIONSHIP

"Dennis and I have been going together for two years. Close to a year ago we decided we'd get married once Dennis passed the law bar. Well, he's passed . . ."

Holly, a twenty-six-year-old medical intern, describes herself as having "cold feet" now that she and Dennis are ready to get married. "Even though I haven't dated another man for over two years and never consciously wanted to, suddenly I'm beginning to wonder if there isn't somebody better out there." Holly feels guilty about her recent interest—or, as she puts it, "curiosity"—in other men. She also complains that neither she nor Dennis seem as involved with each other as they used to be. The romance has grown stagnant, and Holly's worried that this does not bode well for an exciting, involving marriage. Lately, she adds, they've begun arguing a lot over little things.

For all her anxiety about marriage, tears come to Holly's eyes while she's examining the large number of Smartcards she selects for her positive stack. She comments that she'd almost forgotten all the reasons why she fell in love with Dennis and wanted to marry him in the first place. Somehow, she's lost sight of the many positives they have going for them, while she's gotten preoccupied with zeroing in on the few negatives, none of which, she now admits, seems so very important. However, as she delves more deeply into the negative issues—BEING ROMANTIC, EXPRESSING NEEDS, MOOD AND EMOTIONAL ISSUES, and ATTITUDE TOWARD VACATIONS—Holly resolves not to make light of these frictions. "My parents," she says, "always swept issues under the carpet. I thought they were the perfect couple until, when I was fourteen, they very calmly and evenly told me that they were getting divorced."

With the problematic areas of her relationship so concretely laid out, she feels encouraged about working on them with Dennis. "I want to do everything I can to make our marriage work," she declares. Then she looks down at the Smartcards laid out on the table, tapping her stack of positives. "I know that Dennis will too."

♥

"My marriage is going to pieces and I can't seem to do anything about it."

Barbara and Steven have been married for eleven years and have three small children. Lack of time and energy and money problems have taken a toll on their marriage. Barbara is thirty-four, petite, and pretty but there are marked frown lines at the corners of her mouth and she looks weary. While she says that the kids exhaust her emotional resources, it's actually during this past year—a year in which her youngest started full days in school and she's had more time for herself than ever before—that she's felt so depressed about her marriage. "We just don't talk anymore," she complains. When she tries to get Steven to engage in anything more than a superficial conversation, his standard remark is, "I don't know what you want me to talk about." Invariably, Barbara will then bring up an issue that gets her angry and upset. Steven's typical response is, "I don't want to hear it." Barbara describes Steven as being totally wrapped up in his work and unwilling to be bothered with the mundane problems of her life or that of their children.

A fascinating thing happens when Barbara begins laying out the Smartcards. She recognizes how grudging she is about putting any Smartcards on the positive stack. "I really don't want to give Steven any credit, do I?" she muses. When she comes to the card for BEING AFFECTIONATE she stares at it for several moments. "For all my complaints, there really is a lot of affection expressed in our relationship. We always kiss each other and the kids good-night, and the same when everyone takes off in the morning. Some evenings when we watch TV, Steven and I cuddle on the sofa.'' Other positives come to light, but Barbara finds her big stack of negatives ''alarming.'' Some of these negatives she's never discussed with Steven or really never thought much about herself until now. I suggest that she might find the key to her mounting dissatisfaction in those unexplored problems.

After looking over her view of the relationship, we both wonder aloud whether Steven has been seeing things the same way. We decide to invite Steven to put his cards on the table, but I'm concerned that he might feel constrained with Barbara watching. He comes in alone a few days later and takes to the Smartcards rather readily. Looking over his laid-out cards I can see significant similarities with Barbara's sort, and some striking differences. What he finds most astonishing is discovering how many issues there are that he wants to talk about with Barbara. He waves several cards in my direction, a glint in his eye. ''Next time Barbara hounds me to talk, she's in for a big surprise. I've got a lot of things to talk about.'' I suggest that he might even initiate the discussion himself, rather than waiting for Barbara to ''hound him.'' He grins. ''Now that would really blow her mind.''

On many occasions after that, Barbara and Steven did the Smartcards together at my office and at home. Sometimes they selected two or three cards from their negative stacks to discuss, sometimes from their positive stacks, and sometimes they picked out a couple of cards at random—a process that often proved most enlightening. Their experience with the Smartcards revitalized their communication. Problems didn't dissolve, but they were feeling a whole lot closer and full of optimism for the first time in years.

♥

WHEN YOU'VE GOTTEN DIVORCED OR YOU'RE IN THE THROES OF DIVORCE

''Jay was the one who had the affair. He was the bastard. So how come it's me that's left feeling guilty?''

Marsha had been divorced for sixteen months. Taking their four-year-old daughter with her, she left Jay after finding out that he was having an affair with a business colleague. At the time she felt devastated and betrayed. She could not fathom how this could have happened. In their seven years of marriage, she'd always believed that she and Jay had a solid relationship. Later, during the divorce proceedings, her husband, infuriated, told her he'd actually had several brief affairs, the first of which occurred during their first year of marriage.

Marsha is a soft-spoken, engaging woman in her mid-thirties who tells me straight off that she wants to stop feeling so guilty, angry, hurt, and hopeless. "I want to get on with my life, but I feel stuck. I've gone over my marriage for sixteen months now and I still don't understand what went wrong. My family and friends are always telling me it's not my fault and intellectually I believe them. I was completely faithful to Jay. I did everything I could to make him happy. I thought he was . . . happy."

Try as she might, she cannot shake her feeling of guilt—that somehow she wasn't good enough, sexy enough, attractive enough to satisfy her husband. She feels very insecure, especially when it comes to meeting other men. She no longer trusts her judgment; she's terrified of getting hurt again; and she's especially concerned about her four-year-old getting attached to someone she dates.

Marsha is initially cautious about laying out her Smartcards, admitting that she's afraid she'll see in black and white that she really was the one to blame. Nor does she want to end up switching the direction of blame from herself to her husband because that would only fuel the anger and betrayal she's trying to finally put to rest. I explain to her that the beauty of the Smartcard sort is that it doesn't place blame on either party but rather will focus her attention on the issues that either added to or detracted from her marital relationship.

Removing the expectation of blame allows Marsha to do the Smartcard sort with much less anxiety. Very soon, she is completely engrossed, considering each card carefully. She takes nearly an hour to complete the task, making comments as she goes along.

Taking hold of the **FAMILY BACKGROUND ISSUES** card, she remarks that Jay came from a working-class background and his parents were very boisterous and fought a lot. She always sensed that Jay was ashamed of his family. Marsha, the only child of a professional couple, has always been very close to her parents. "I wanted to model my own marriage after theirs, but I never really took into account before now how very different Jay is from my dad." She points to several cards to emphasize this point: **HANDLING CRISES, CONTROL/LEADERSHIP**

ISSUES, and DECISION MAKING. Whereas Marsha's parents always worked together as a team, Jay insisted on being the one in charge.

For a long time, Marsha admits, she liked Jay's take-charge attitude. She interpreted that as an indication that he enjoyed taking care of her. Marsha thinks about this some more and comes to another insight. Maybe she's not as much like her mother as she always thought she was.

Marsha looks at the stack of problem areas she's laid down on the table and flushes, confessing that she never discussed most of these issues with Jay for fear of "upsetting the apple cart." She was so invested in having a "perfect marriage" that she sacrificed having a "real relationship." She thinks that Jay played into this charade as well because he wanted a marriage that was the opposite of his parents'. For a marriage that lasted seven years, there are a surprising number of unknowns—more issues that she and Jay never discussed. "We really didn't communicate very much."

After Marsha puts her Smartcards on the table, she looks up. There's a bittersweet smile on her face. "We never really did mesh, Jay and I. We had such different outlooks on so many issues. And so many went totally unexplored. I really allowed the things that were important to me to get shoved under the rug. I think Jay probably did the same." Her smile brightens. "Okay, so neither of us was to blame. We both made bad choices for us." She gathers up the Smartcards and asks if she can keep them because she wants to go into the next relationship she has "with my eyes wide open."

CHAPTER THREE

PUTTING YOUR SMARTCARDS ON THE TABLE

The deck of sixty-six Smartcards contains the sum of the significant issues in a relationship. Each Smartcard represents one aspect of a relationship that can be important in itself as well as having a significant effect on the whole. Imagine that your relationship is a large circle. If you laid the Smartcards like a patchwork over the circle, they would blanket the territory completely, overlapping here and there to make sure that every space was covered.

♥

THE SMARTCARD MIND-SET

There is a special way I want you to think about each Smartcard before you decide where to place it. Focus first and foremost on the overall role the issue itself plays within your relationship. As a couple, consider how well or poorly you handle or deal with each issue. Are the two of you compatible; do you see eye-to-eye on the issue? Is this issue a positive feature in your relationship? If there are differences in the way each of you views or copes with a particular issue, are you comfortable with the

29

differences or do these differences raise doubts, create tension, and/or cause arguments—i.e., is it a negative feature? Because a relationship involves how both of you behave and react toward each other, it is crucially important, as you look at each card, to see each other interactively: how successful or unsuccessful are you as a couple in each particular arena of your relationship? When problems do come up, do you resolve them satisfactorily? By first looking at the relationship as its own entity, you gain perspective on how your partnership is working. Then step back and think about the part that each of you plays in making this a positive feature or a negative factor in your relationship.

In thinking about those issues that are negatives, *do not* let yourself fall into the seductive trap of making judgments about your partner. Accusations and laying blame won't help you fully explore how each of you contributes to a problem and what you both might do to improve the situation. Judgments close you off, distance you from your partner, and prevent an open and honest evaluation of the problem.

It will be helpful, when you do your Smartcard sort, to refer to the Questions section in Chapter Five (see reference guide on page 48), if you need help in thinking through the levels of meaning of a particular issue, getting a better understanding of what a particular issue involves, and exploring it in greater depth before deciding where it belongs.

Marion is doing a Smartcard sort about her relationship with her husband, Tony, and is deciding which stack to put the HAVING SEX card on. She correctly focuses first on the overall role sex plays in their relationship. Has their sexual experience brought them closer together, increased their happiness? For the moment she puts off considering whether either is a sexual dynamo. She factors in their individual contributions a moment later and decides to place the HAVING SEX on her positive stack.

When Marion comes to the LISTENING card, she pauses. "I know I'm not supposed to start making judgments about Tony, but this is my biggest gripe with him. He never listens." She places the card in the negative stack. When she refers to the questions that delve into this issue, she is able to see that she contributes to the problem as well. She's been so focused on how lousy a listener Tony is that she hasn't spent much time thinking about how much and how well she listens to him. She also realizes that she's so sure he'll turn her off, that she takes a defensive stance every time she brings up a subject with him. Is she setting herself up to be tuned out?

You should take caution to avoid ending up choosing where to place Smartcards based solely on what you like or dislike about your partner. A relationship is the unique product of what *two* individuals have together—what you have created together that you wouldn't have apart. Take **HAVING FUN**. Marion describes Tony as a fun-loving guy, and adds that she's "far from a stick-in-the-mud." They're both into having fun, but they don't often have fun together. The problem is that Tony's idea of fun is going to parties, ball games, action movies. Marion prefers romantic dinners for two, hiking, playing tennis. While she sees them both as open to having a good time and very positive about having fun, this card is a negative because they haven't figured out enough ways to have fun together. Quite the opposite, Marion realizes now, they have no fun together. Although this issue has been a stumbling block for them, they've both drifted into accepting the situation as a given rather than trying to come up with new and innovative ways they can have fun as a couple.

On a rare occasion a quality of your partner may be so objectionable, so upsetting in and of itself, that it proves deeply disturbing. Take Frank, who's a very successful gun manufacturer. He's loving, tender, attentive, works banker's hours, but Carol hates what he does for a living; in a sense, hates him for doing it. As Carol looks through her Smartcard sort for the first time, she seizes upon the **ATTITUDE ABOUT MORALITY** card, taps it on the table, and frowns. In her personal relationship with Frank they have no morality issues. Everything they do when they are together suits Carol's moral value system to a "t." But she finds the immorality of Frank's profession so offensive that she must follow her deepest sensibilities and put the **ATTITUDE ABOUT MORALITY** Smartcard high in her negative stack.

♥

GETTING DOWN TO BUSINESS

Begin putting your cards on the table. Take up your first Smartcard and place it in front of you in one of four spots:

Sorted Smartcard Stacks

POSITIVES   NEGATIVES   UNKNOWNS   DISCARDS

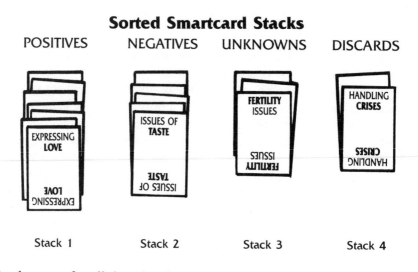

Stack 1   Stack 2   Stack 3   Stack 4

Do the same for all the other Smartcards. Read through the descriptions and explanations below to get a firm grasp on the criteria for each stack.

STACK ONE
Positive features of the relationship

Sort through the Smartcards and separate out the ones that reflect what's right, what's working well in your relationship. Again, refer to the Questions section in Chapter Five if you want more information on any card.

For example, Bill has been going out with Judy for four months. He's wildly in love with her, but he has some anxiety about the relationship. He fans out the Smartcard deck in his hand and starts picking out positive issue cards. These are the first five he chooses: HAVING SEX, HAVING A SENSE OF HUMOR, ATTITUDE TOWARD WORK AND EARNING A LIVING, ENERGY LEVEL ISSUES, BEING ROMANTIC.

Here's how Bill evaluated these positives:

HAVING SEX—He and Judy have sex frequently and lovingly. Their sexual experiences together make them feel very close. They initiate with just about equal frequency. He feels confident that they both enjoy the sexual part of their relationship a lot.

HAVING A SENSE OF HUMOR—He highly values humor in a relationship so he's very invested in rating the humor issue. Some women have not gotten his sense of humor, which has been very frustrating. He has a dry sense of humor whereas Judy's is broader, but he feels these differences complement each other. They end up having lots of laughs together. HAVING A SENSE OF HUMOR is a strong plus in this relationship.

ATTITUDE TOWARD WORK—Bill's work as an ad exec is very central to his identity and he devotes a great deal of time to it. Judy, a free-lance illustrator, has a looser work style and isn't nearly as concerned with personal achievement, but her attitude doesn't extend to him. In the past, Bill has had conflicts with dates who were as intense about work as he was. There was a lot of competition. Ironically, in this instance, an issue makes it to the positive stack because of their differences.

ENERGY LEVEL ISSUES—He and Judy are both high-energy people and this is a significant plus for Bill, who finds that low-energy people bring him down.

BEING ROMANTIC—Bill enjoys Judy's appreciation when he brings her flowers or gifts, sends her cute cards, and takes her to romantic spots. She has written some beautiful poems and they both enjoy curling up and having Judy read them to him. Bill thinks this kind of romance is vital to staying in love and a key to a good relationship, so the BEING ROMANTIC Smartcard will be high on his positive stack.

STACK TWO
Negative or troubling features of the relationship

Stack Two is for issues that provoke unhappy feelings or represent subjects of tension, problem areas or sources of misery or despair.

Jane has been married to Larry for fifteen years and lately she's been arguing with him over money. She's grown almost obsessed about their financial situation and it's become the primary focus of her marital complaints. At first, all she can pick for the negative stack is the Smartcard labeled HANDLING MONEY. I encourage her to take a second run-through and she begins selecting other cards as well for the negative, or problematic, stack—BEING AFFECTIONATE and HAVING CONVERSATIONS are two out of many that end up there.

BEING AFFECTIONATE—In selecting this card for the negative stack Jane is reminding herself how she's lost sight of the importance of this issue over the years—and how long she's gone without the tenderness she once cherished. It's not just a case of Larry no longer being affectionate enough because she, too, has stopped putting much time or effort into this area of their relationship.

HAVING CONVERSATIONS—One thing Jane used to love about their relationship was that she and Larry talked a lot, and that communication between them made her feel closer to him. Over the past few years this activity has fallen by the wayside because neither of them has made time for it. Fighting has become their way of communicating.

STACK THREE
Unknowns

When you don't know enough to decide whether an issue is a positive or a negative, put its Smartcard in the stack you've created for unknowns.

The Smartcards that you place in this stack will turn out to be especially significant if you're exploring a new relationship. Early on there is a tendency to overestimate how much you know about your partner and your relationship. It's all too easy to overlook important issues because you're spending so much time having fun together that you can't be bothered. Take a good look at your unknown stack—ignoring too many issues can lead to some very bad long-term choices.

If you're evaluating an ongoing relationship of any notable duration, try hard to find issues for your unknown stack. You don't want to take the relationship for granted and ignore the effects of the inevitable changes and transformations that take place over time. New positives and negatives crop up due to such events as career changes, retirement, changes in family composition, moving to a new area, or individual growth, and even as the natural result of aging—all of which alter you, your partner, and the nature of your intimate relationship.

Paula has been living with Doug for six years and they're planning to get married. The Smartcard sort allows Paula to identify all the areas they'll need to talk about to be ready for the big changes ahead. Paula is surprised to discover how many issues have taken on new meaning now that they are getting married, among them ATTITUDE TOWARD EDUCATION, RELIGIOUS ISSUES, ATTITUDE TOWARD HOME AND HOME CARE.

ATTITUDE TOWARD EDUCATION—Paula is thinking of one day going back to college for an advanced degree and realizes that she and Doug have never even discussed this issue. She has no idea of Doug's attitude about her future schooling, nor has she thought about or discussed its financial or social ramifications on their married life.

RELIGIOUS ISSUES—Although she and Doug are from different religious denominations, the difference has never been a problem. When they do go to services they take turns visiting each other's church. However, now that they're getting married they have to face the question of what religion they'll raise children in.

ATTITUDE TOWARD HOME AND HOME CARE—So far they've been living in Paula's apartment, so she'd made most of the important decisions about the place before they got together. Once they're married, though, Paula wants to consider buying a home. She has almost no idea what Doug thinks about cost or locations, how they'll furnish it, who'll be responsible for different chores around the house, and so on.

STACK FOUR
Discards

This stack is for issues that seem to have no relevance to your relationship. Any issue that doesn't fit into the other three stacks belongs here. A large discard stack may underscore your naiveté about relationships in general, or may glaringly highlight the shallowness of your current relationship.

Remember Seth, the twenty-year-old college student in Chapter Two? When he did a Smartcard sort on Leslie, the girl of his dreams, most of the cards ended up in his discard stack. Seth was typical of many of the young people who have done the Smartcard sort. They started by thinking there were really just a few key issues at play in making a good relationship—the primary ones being having sex, having fun, and personal appearance. Like Seth, they were surprised, in some cases astonished, at how many factors could go into making up a deep and substantive relationship. The Smartcard sort became more than an examination of their current relationships. It also provided a learning experience, greatly expanding their conceptual framework for thinking about relationships in general.

When too many discards show up for an involvement you're pretty serious about, it usually means you have a long way to go to understand what makes up a successful relationship.

Gail, a pediatrician, has been dating a colleague for nearly six months. Before she starts her Smartcard sort she tells me that she and Leon have a very close, satisfactory relationship, but there are a few problems. After doing her Smartcard sort, however, it turns out to be not the few problems that catch her attention and mine, but her large number of discards. To highlight just a "few," these include: HANDLING MONEY, HANDLING CRISES, SETTING GOALS, FAMILY BACKGROUND ISSUES, SEXISM ISSUES, FERTILITY ISSUES, ATTITUDE TOWARD HOME AND HOME CARE, MARITAL STATUS ISSUES, RELATIONSHIPS WITH PARENTS AND IN-LAWS, ATTITUDE TOWARD VACATIONS, and ATTITUDE TOWARD PAST RELATIONSHIPS.

At first, Gail claims these issues are unimportant because she and Leon are both very independent people and neither of them has any interest in marriage at this time. But as she goes through these discards, she begins to wonder if she is intentionally distancing herself from Leon because she is afraid of getting too close, too involved. She raises this possibility: "Maybe I'm scared I'll discover I really do want to get married and Leon really doesn't. By casting these issues aside, I'm playing it safe. But am I in the kind of relationship I really want to be in?"

Discards become very interesting to review when compared to how much they change over time, or compared to discards from another relationship. Issues that seem to be of no consequence at first may turn out to be crucial later on.

Greta compared her Smartcard sort from before and during her marriage to Josh. Many of her discards from her first sort moved into the other three stacks in her second sort. WATCHING TV was never an issue before she and Josh were married, but now that they are "settled down," Greta complains that Josh has become a couch potato and all his television time drives her crazy. Since they didn't live together before they were married, ATTITUDE TOWARD HOME AND HOME CARE also found its way into her discard pile during her first sort. In her second sort, she places this card in her positive stack. Shortly after they were married, Greta and Josh bought an old brownstone that they intended to renovate themselves. "Everyone warned us it would be the end of our marriage, but we had the best time fixing our place up. We not only worked well together," Greta says, "but we discovered we had much more similar tastes than we would have guessed. We learned a lot about each other and grew closer together while we were sawing boards and hammering all those nails."

The discard stack can prove enlightening when you review your discards from several sorts. Do the same discards always show up? Are they really as unimportant as you think? Do you habitually underestimate the importance of certain critical issues? Even though we call them discards, these cards can actually provide you with a wealth of information.

CHAPTER FOUR

REFINING THE STACKS AND RANKING YOUR SMARTCARDS

You now should have four stacks in front of you: positives, negatives, unknowns, and discards.

If you have more than ten positives, subdivide the stack in two: Reserve one stack for really great features, and place the remainder of your positives in the other stack.

From your negative stack, no matter what its size, sort out three subdivisions: minor problem areas, serious negatives, and fatal flaws (intensely painful issues, unforgivable defects, monstrously upsetting problems). Fatal flaws represent unresolved problem areas that can, on their own, destroy your love relationship.

If your stack of unknowns is bigger than ten cards, create a smaller stack of those unknowns that you think are most important to know more about.

Your discards will not be subdivided.

Next, you will be laying out your Smartcards, subdivision by subdivision, in descending order of importance. As if playing a game of solitaire, lay your Smartcards out overlapping vertically, starting at the top with the most important issue and moving down from there.

Ranked Smartcard Stacks

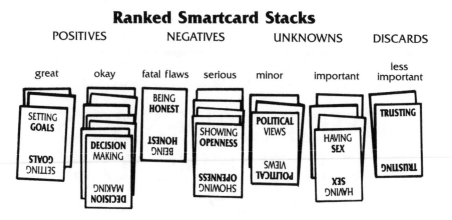

Note: discards are not ranked

Bill ranked his really great features stack of Smartcards in this order: HAVING A SENSE OF HUMOR topped his list, then HAVING SEX, BEING ROMANTIC, ATTITUDE TOWARD WORK AND EARNING A LIVING, and ENERGY LEVEL ISSUES followed in that order.

Jane ranked her significant negative stack in this order: EXPRESSING LOVE topped her list, followed by HAVING CONVERSATIONS, HANDLING MONEY, and BEING INVOLVED IN SPORTS in that order.

Paula ranked her unknowns in this order: ETHNIC/CULTURAL/SOCIAL/SPIRITUAL/RELIGIOUS VALUES topped her list, followed by ATTITUDE TOWARD HOME AND HOME CARE and ATTITUDE TOWARD EDUCATION.

♥

INTERPRETING YOUR SMARTCARD SORT

Your Smartcards are on the table, sorted out and rank ordered from most to least positive or negative. If you've laid them out carefully overlapping like solitaire cards, as in the illustration above, you'll be able to see all the issue headings.

Begin by looking at the plus side of your relationship. It's good for your morale and should help keep your attitude balanced. You want to avoid the obvious path of seeing only the bad points and becoming unduly discouraged.

Starting with your positives, answer the following general questions for each of the categories. Consider your problem areas and especially your fatal flaws very carefully. In the same way, be careful not to make light of the positives you value greatly.

Examine your POSITIVES

Are your top-ranked Smartcards the features you value most in a relationship, or are important positives missing from this stack?

Are there any cards among the positives that you didn't expect?

Are you surprised at how many or how few positives you see?

♥

Examine your NEGATIVES

How troubling are these negatives?

Were you aware of these negatives prior to sorting the Smartcards?

Have you tried in the past to deal with these negatives in any constructive way?

If there are negatives you are seeing for the first time, do you see ways to deal with and/or resolve them?

How do the negatives compare with your positives? Is there a good enough balance to warrant continued work on the relationship?

♥

TAKE YOUR FATAL FLAWS STACK VERY SERIOUSLY

The prospect of a fatal flaw in a relationship is so grave that it's not talked or written about much. It's very hard to face the reality that just one failing area of an intimate relationship could doom the whole thing—but it definitely can. Many's the time I've treated a couple for years only to have them break up over an original flaw that one of them could simply not abide.

For example, Jesse hates Margie's extremely intrusive mother and Margie can't live without speaking to her mother daily and complaining all about Jesse. Harriet spends too much money, too often, without consulting Ned. Alex has a serious gambling habit that Christine can't tolerate. These aren't fatal flaws for every couple, but all of them have been fatal flaws for some of the couples I've treated.

Fatal flaws cause considerable pain. Even a large number of highly valued Smartcards in your positive stack cannot compensate for truly fatal flaws. The operative word here is *fatal*. A relationship with *unalterable* fatal flaws is doomed to create endless misery.

Unfortunately, in the throes of romantic love, most people would rather not acknowledge or even consider the possibility of fatal flaws, but if you make the choice to face them early on, you can save yourself a great deal of pain and sorrow down the line. Remember Meg, who was so infatuated with Brian that she didn't want to acknowledge that there were some serious problems in her relationship? After doing the Smartcard sort, Meg allowed herself to admit that a lack of trust and reliability could prove to be fatal flaws in her relationship with Brian if these issues couldn't be resolved. Not long after that, Meg decided to break off her involvement with Brian when she concluded that she was "just whistling Dixie" to think she could change him.

♥

Examine your unknowns

Expect to find a large number of Smartcards here if your relationship is relatively new, no matter how much in love you are and how accepting you feel about your partner.

Would it matter if you didn't ever know much about any of these issues? If your answer is yes, decide which issues you need to explore more fully.

Do you recognize some of these issues as questions that you've deliberately avoided exploring? Ask yourself why.

Do you feel confident of finding the answers to these questions in the natural course of your relationship? How would that come about?

If there are a lot of issues in this stack, what does this say to you about the depth of your relationship?

Examine your discards

Now that you think about it, have you placed any Smartcards here that are actually significant parts of your relationship? If so, place them where they really belong.

What do your discards tell you about the nature of your relationship? If there are a large number, do they indicate that you are really just involved in a friendship, or a short-term affair, or that you're not really invested in the relationship, or that you have a superficial view of intimate relationships? Be searchingly honest here. This is where you get the opportunity to stop misleading yourself—and your partner.

♥

Based on your answers to the questions for each of the stacks you've laid out, you'll have a strong sense of the strengths and weaknesses of your relationship. You'll have discovered many features and flaws that you've failed to acknowledge before, and you'll have raised some issues in your own mind that you will want to consider more carefully or explore with your partner. The next step is to make a record of the actual layout of your card sort.

♥

RECORDING YOUR RESULTS

Fill out the worksheet (one set is provided on the following pages) so that you can review your Smartcard sort at a later date. Each worksheet has space for recording several different card sorts. Using your worksheet as a base, you can make comparisons with future Smartcard sorts to see how your relationship is progressing. It will also be helpful to compare that worksheet with others if you become involved in a new relationship.

The worksheet is very easy to fill out. At the top, in the first column write in your partner's name and the date you did the sort. Each Smartcard is listed down the left-hand side of the page, alphabetized by its highlighted key word and numbered to correspond to your Smartcards. Next to each issue heading you simply record the stack you chose and the rank you assigned each Smartcard. Place a plus (+) in the stack box if that issue falls in the positives stack, a minus (-) for the negatives stack, a question mark (?) for your unknowns, or an X for your discards. Number the order of your ranking next to each of your signs, using 1 for the top Smartcard of each stack and working your way down.

Here's how Bill recorded his top positives:

33. HAVING A SENSE OF **HUMOR**	+ 1	(his highest positive)
55. HAVING **SEX**	+ 2	

These are Jane's top negatives:

37. EXPRESSING **LOVE**	− 1	(her highest negative)
13. HAVING **CONVERSATIONS**	− 2	

Paula's unknowns:

65. ETHNIC/CULTURAL/SOCIAL/SPIRITUAL/RELIGIOUS **VALUES**	? 1	
31. ATTITUDE TOWARD **HOME** AND HOME CARE	? 2	

Gail's discards:

60. ISSUES OF **TASTE**	X	(no ranking)
40. HANDLING **MONEY**	X	

SMARTCARDS WORKSHEET

Score each issue as follows: + for each positive, − for each negative, ? for each unknown, X for each discard. List ranking next to each sign. Use 1 for highest ranking. Don't rank discards.

ISSUE	NAME/DATE	NAME/DATE	NAME/DATE	NAME/DATE	NAME/DATE	NAME/DATE
1. BEING **AFFECTIONATE**						
2. ATTITUDE TOWARD **AGE** AND AGING						
3. **ANXIETY** LEVEL ISSUES						
4. PERSONAL **APPEARANCE**						
5. **ARGUING** AND FIGHTING						
6. USING **BIRTH CONTROL**						
7. **CARING** ABOUT OTHER PEOPLE						
8. ISSUES IN HAVING OR RAISING **CHILDREN**						
9. MAKING A **COMMITMENT** TO THE RELATIONSHIP						
10. **COMMUNICATING**						
11. BEING **CONSIDERATE**						
12. **CONTROL**/LEADERSHIP ISSUES						
13. HAVING **CONVERSATIONS**						
14. BEING **COOPERATIVE** AND SHARING						
15. HANDLING **CRISES**						
16. **DECISION** MAKING						
17. USING/ABUSING **DRUGS** AND ALCOHOL						
18. ATTITUDE TOWARD **EDUCATION**						
19. EXPRESSING **EMOTIONAL** HONESTY						
20. **ENERGY** LEVEL ISSUES						

ISSUE	NAME/DATE	NAME/DATE	NAME/DATE	NAME/DATE	NAME/DATE	NAME/DATE	NAME/DATE
21. **FAMILY** BACKGROUND ISSUES							
22. EXPRESSING **FEELINGS**/HAVING FEELINGS							
23. **FERTILITY** ISSUES							
24. ATTITUDE TOWARD **FOOD** AND EATING							
25. ATTITUDE TOWARD **FRIENDSHIP**							
26. HAVING **FUN**							
27. SETTING **GOALS**							
28. **HABITS**							
29. **HEALTH** ISSUES							
30. **HOBBIES** AND OUTSIDE INTERESTS							
31. ATTITUDE TOWARD **HOME** AND HOME CARE							
32. BEING **HONEST**							
33. HAVING A SENSE OF **HUMOR**							
34. PERSONAL **HYGIENE** ISSUES							
35. **LEGAL** ISSUES							
36. **LISTENING**							
37. EXPRESSING **LOVE**							
38. **MARITAL** STATUS ISSUES							
39. **MENTAL** HEALTH ISSUES							
40. HANDLING **MONEY**							
41. **MOOD** AND EMOTIONAL ISSUES							
42. ATTITUDE ABOUT **MORALITY**							
43. EXPRESSING **NEEDS**							
44. SHOWING **OPENNESS**							

ISSUE	NAME/DATE	NAME/DATE	NAME/DATE	NAME/DATE	NAME/DATE	NAME/DATE
45. RELATIONSHIPS WITH **PARENTS** AND IN-LAWS						
46. ATTITUDE TOWARD **PAST RELATIONSHIPS**						
47. CARING FOR/ABOUT **PETS** AND PLANTS						
48. HAVING **PHYSICAL** SKILLS						
49. BEING **POLITE**/CORDIAL						
50. **POLITICAL** VIEWS						
51. **PROBLEM-SOLVING** STYLE, ATTITUDE, AND ABILITY						
52. BEING **REASONABLE** AND FAIR						
53. BEING **RELIABLE**						
54. BEING **ROMANTIC**						
55. HAVING **SEX**						
56. **SEXISM** ISSUES						
57. HAVING **SOCIAL SKILLS**						
58. BEING INVOLVED IN **SPORTS**						
59. BEING **SUPPORTIVE**						
60. ISSUES OF **TASTE**						
61. ATTITUDE TOWARD **TIME**						
62. **TRUSTING**						
63. WATCHING **TV**						
64. ATTITUDE TOWARD **VACATIONS**						
65. ETHNIC/CULTURAL/SOCIAL/SPIRITUAL/RELIGIOUS **VALUES**						
66. ATTITUDE TOWARD **WORK** AND EARNING A LIVING						

CHAPTER FIVE

THE SMARTCARD QUESTIONS

DELVING DEEPER

Having done your Smartcard sort and rankings, here is your opportunity to further explore your most significant issues: positives, negatives, and unknowns.

On the following pages we've included a series of thought-provoking questions for each of the Smartcards, to help you probe and clarify the meaning *you* give to each one. Your goal for this activity should be self-exploration—creating a record of your thoughts, responses, and reactions to all the parts of a relationship that are significant for you.

Take the time to organize your ideas fully enough to jot them down in the space provided after each question. You may also want to go beyond a given space and keep a record in your own journal.

1. BEING **AFFECTIONATE**

In what ways do your expressions of mutual affection enhance your relationship?

Are your needs for affection being met by each other? If not, what's missing? Which areas are especially lacking in affection? When are the two of you least affectionate? The most affectionate?

Do you think you and your partner have the same needs for affection? What are the differences? Are you an out-and-out mismatch in terms of affection?

Have you and your partner been able to make improvements in the past in areas where affection was lacking? Does it seem likely that you could have more affection together in the future? Are you both willing to make some changes?

What is the minimum level of affection which you could tolerate?

2. ATTITUDE TOWARD **AGE** AND AGING

If there's a significant age gap, how much does it matter to you? To your partner? How will if affect you in the future?

How does your partner's attitude toward his/her age and yours affect the relationship?

How do your attitudes toward age and aging affect the kind of things you do and don't do?

How does your attitude toward age and aging affect the decisions you make or don't make as a couple?

What insecurities or fears arise out of the prospect of growing old together?

3. ANXIETY LEVEL ISSUES

What do you do when you become anxious? Do you talk it out, act it out positively (e.g., play a sport) or negatively (e.g., use drugs or alcohol), imagine catastrophes, deny that anything is wrong, withdraw emotionally, minimize feelings, become depressed and immobilized, take it out on yourself or your partner?

How does your partner act when he or she is anxious?

How do you act toward each other when either of you becomes anxious?

What kind of support does your partner provide you with when you're anxious? Is it what you want? Is it enough?

How could your partner best help you when you become anxious?

Are your expectations reasonable? Are your partner's?

What issues make each of you the most anxious?

♥

4. PERSONAL **APPEARANCE**

Do you like each other's personal appearance? How important is this to the relationship?

If there are aspects of each other's personal appearance that you don't like, can you discuss them?

Is personal appearance of equal or differing importance to each of you?

Do either you or your partner feel the other's appearance is inappropriate to your age, social status, career, certain situations, etc.?

Do you or your partner care what other people think about the other's personal appearance?

What good or bad aspects of personal appearance could blind you to your partner's shortcomings or strengths and talents?

How does your attitude toward your own and your partner's personal appearance (and that of others) affect your life, your relationship, your health or career?

How does your partner's attitude toward your and his or her personal appearance (and that of others) affect your partner's life, your relationship, your health or career?

♥

5. ARGUING AND FIGHTING

How do you and your partner resolve your differences? Do you fight or argue at all?

What are the issues around which you and your partner fight the most? The least?

What do you and your partner avoid or fear fighting over?

Do you fight over everything you disagree about? Do either of you ever let something pass?

Are things better or worse after you fight?

How do you fight and argue? Do your styles differ (e.g., yelling, silent treatment, confrontational, blaming, being derogatory, name calling, intellectualizing, discussing calmly, getting heated)?

When you are at a complete impasse, how do you handle it?

Can either of you own up to being wrong?

Does the fighting stop only because one of you gave in? How much room is there for compromise? By you? By your partner?

What rules do you and your partner have for fighting clean (e.g., setting time and subject limits)? If you don't have any, what rules would you like to have?

If the fighting has ever become physical, how have you and your partner handled this? Do either of you have a past history of getting physical in fights?

Do you each take responsibility for examining how past experiences are influencing current disagreements (e.g., do you fight about the same issues your parents fought about, the same issues you fought about in past relationships, etc.)?

♥

6. USING **BIRTH CONTROL**

How does using (or not using) birth control affect your sex life?

How open are you and your partner to discussing the nitty-gritty basics of safe sex and contraception?

Are you comfortable or at odds about who takes the responsibility for birth control?

Is either of you careless? How does this affect your relationship?

What are each of your attitudes toward birth control? Before you had (have) sex, did (will) you discuss what you'd do about pregnancy? Have you had this conversation yet? Is there conflict or consensus?

♥

7. CARING ABOUT OTHER PEOPLE

How aware are each of you of other people's needs? Do you have conflicts over differences in your caring styles?

How often do each of you spend time caring for other people instead of caring for yourselves or each other?

Do either or both of you spend time rescuing or doing things for others that they could do for themselves?

Are either of you overly or inappropriately concerned for others at the expense of your relationship?

Do you display as much concern for each other as you do for others?

Do either of you demand or accept inappropriate displays of caring from others?

♥

8. ISSUES IN HAVING OR RAISING **CHILDREN**

Is having children—or not having children—a source of happiness or unhappiness in your relationship?

Do you agree or disagree on whether or not to have children? On the number of children you'd want?

Are you and your partner at different stages of life so that the question of having children might become a serious conflict (e.g., one of you has children from a past relationship and wants no more, the pressure of the biological clock, you want kids and your partner wants to retire or feel free to travel or to devote time and energy to other activities, etc.)?

If you already have children from this relationship or another, do you agree on whether or not to have any more?

If you're in a serious dating relationship or married without kids, have you talked a lot about having children and compared your child-rearing ideas? Are you in sync? Are there conflicts? Is this a warning sign?

What areas of conflict do you have in raising your children together? How do you settle those conflicts?

If you have children with special needs, handicaps, problems, do you have an approach to helping the child that you agree upon? Has coping with the child's difficulties brought you closer together, farther apart?

How were each of you raised? Are either of you intent on repeating your parents' child-rearing practices? On *not* repeating them?

♥

9. MAKING A **COMMITMENT** TO THE RELATIONSHIP

Do you have a committed relationship? If not, why not?

Are you happy with the degree of commitment you have?

Do you ever talk about commitment? Do you both mean the same thing when you do? How do you each define your commitment to this relationship?

How do you see the future of the relationship—long-term, short-term?

Has your partner been able to make commitments in the past (marriage, lovers, friends, family, work, education, etc.)? Have you? How much do you know about your partner's past commitments? How do you feel about them?

To what lengths are you each willing to go in order to fulfill your commitments?

Are you and your partner open to discussing why you can't or won't make a commitment?

If your partner can't or won't make a commitment, what are you going to do about it (e.g., set a time limit for a decision, do nothing now, end the relationship, seek professional help)?

♥

10. COMMUNICATING

How well do each of you communicate needs, wants, fears, hopes, dreams, victories, defeats?

Can you talk about differences or problems without always ending up in an argument?

What words best express your communication styles (e.g., verbal, nonverbal, avoids, confronts, conceals, open, hostile, accusatory, indirect, direct, fearful, deceitful, dominates and controls, expresses self well or poorly, confuses or is confused, cynical, apologetic, bargains, realistic, unrealistic, angry, withholding, punitive, etc.)?

If the communication in your relationship is primarily limited to small talk about mundane matters like daily management and making arrangements, how well do you do in that area?

What portion of your communication is devoted to straightening out misunderstandings? Which misunderstandings happen most frequently? Why?

Are you tolerant of the differences between your styles of communicating?

Are you aware of and do you share your feelings about each other's nonverbal communications?

How do you know what is on your partner's mind if he or she is not a great communicator? Are you guided by other people's feedback? Do you resort to anger and confrontation? Do you feel like you're getting mixed messages?

Do you avoid asking about what your partner is thinking or feeling for fear of retaliation or rejection; losing face, or status, or control; being thought of as interfering, meddling, stubborn, or manipulative? Why and how? What's the case with your partner?

Are you willing to go outside of the relationship in order to obtain help to understand communication breakdown and to gain some new skills?

♥

11. BEING **CONSIDERATE**

Do you go out of your way for each other?

Are you able to put your partner first (sometimes, frequently, too often, never)? How about your partner?

Do you take each other into account before making decisions?

Do you try not to hurt each other's feelings unnecessarily?

Do you respect each other's property?

How do you show consideration for each other's needs and interests?

How considerate are you of each other's tastes, styles, physical comfort, activities?

♥

12. CONTROL/LEADERSHIP ISSUES

Over what areas, if any, do you battle for control?

Do either of you control conversation or situations by changing the subject, refusing to discuss the issue, silent treatment, cutting the other person off, displaying anger, shouting down the other person, walking out, bullying?

Are difficult situations and crises controlled by high emotions and drama such as threats to end the relationship, tears, hanging up the phone, walking out, shouting?

Have you noticed any gender and/or ethnic differences around control issues?

Do either of you experience a feeling of loss of control if the other person does something better, points out an error, has a different opinion or viewpoint, wants to do something differently, criticizes?

How do each of you feel when you need to relinquish control to the other (e.g., when your partner drives, makes social plans for you, arranges vacations; when you are sick or incapacitated)?

Do you and/or your partner ever resort to violence or the threat of violence? What feelings and problems has this caused? Have you sought professional and legal help?

Is your relationship controlled by sex, alcohol, work, drugs, gambling, or other forms of addiction?

How much is your need (your partner's need) to control a sign of your (your partner's) insecurity, lack of trust, unwillingness to get close, etc.?

Are your control issues complicated enough so that you could benefit from some counseling?

♥

13. HAVING **CONVERSATIONS**

Are conversations an important part of your relationship?

Do your conversations bring you closer together?

Do you both like to chat, share ideas and opinions? To the same degree? If not, how does this affect your relationship?

Do you have conversations that lead to better understanding of each other? How often? Do you like having them? What is their importance to your relationship?

Can you listen to each other's problems without feeling that you have to solve the problem?

Who usually initiates serious topics of conversation? Is this okay with both of you?

Do you like to have conversations at the same times or does it always seem like one of you wants to talk when the other doesn't?

In serious conversations do you take the time to clarify exactly what each of you means to be saying?

Do your serious, or casual, conversations degenerate into fights?

Do you talk about topics that you don't see eye-to-eye on?

Do you have conversations just for the fun of it?

Can you identify what patterns you have in your styles that are a help or a hindrance to having successful conversations?

Are you aware of conversational differences with regard to male/female style, ethnic or age differences?

♥

14. BEING **COOPERATIVE** AND SHARING

Can you cooperate with each other to solve a problem or to complete a task? If not, why can't you?

Can you share and take turns at leadership?

Can you pull together at times of stress and crisis?

As a couple, what problems do you have cooperating and sharing with others (at work, play, with friends, other family members)?

Are you and your partner both clear about how the other defines cooperating and sharing? Do your definitions mesh?

Are there areas that pose particular problems around sharing and cooperating? What are they? Do you understand why they're a problem? Are you emotionally open to exploring what part you are playing in the problem?

How fairly do you share information, time, work, obligations?

How can you work together to find new solutions to old problems?

15. HANDLING **CRISES**

How well or poorly do you work together as a team in time of crisis? Do you pull closer together or grow farther apart during and/or after?

How do you each react and respond when facing crises?

What types of crises have you faced together and how successful were you at it?

Are you facing a serious crisis now or is there one brewing? How are you handling or preparing for it?

Do you or your partner tend to minimize the significance or severity of the crisis? Is your partner helpful and thoughtful, or overbearing and controlling? How does he or she make the circumstances worse or better?

16. DECISION MAKING

How do you come to decisions that affect the relationship (e.g., by yourselves, with help from each other or others, impulsively, after careful deliberation, by consensus)?

If your suggestions and opinions aren't considered when the decision affects both of you, how do you feel and react?

In what areas are your decisions collaborative? Unilateral? How do you feel about this?

As a couple, which are the most difficult areas in which to reach decisions?

How do your own decision-making tactics affect your relationship?

When decisions involving you have to be made, what method do you have for making them? Do you involve your partner? What are the ground rules? What would you like them to be?

What's the emotional component of making decisions together? Is it fun and interesting, or difficult and stressful? How can you each improve the process?

♥

17. USING/ABUSING **DRUGS** AND ALCOHOL

Is drug or alcohol use a significant aspect of your relationship?

Is your (your partner's) current drug/alcohol use acceptable to each of you?

If alcohol/drug use is a problem, are you each willing to talk openly about it? Seek help?

How does your (your partner's) use of alcohol/drugs affect job, friends, family?

Are there any emotional problems caused by drug/alcohol use that affect your relationship negatively and might be helped by some form of therapy?

Are either of you aiding or abetting the other's abuse of drugs and alcohol?

If you (your partner) used to be a heavy user, or addicted, when did you (your partner) stop? Are either of you currently involved in any counseling or self-help programs?

What affect has past drug/alcohol use had on your partner's or your health? Was there satisfactory treatment?

If there's a serious drug or alcohol abuse problem that your partner will not change, are you willing to end the relationship for your own good?

♥

18. ATTITUDE TOWARD **EDUCATION**

What are the educational differences between you and your partner, and how do these differences affect your life together?

What impact will differing attitudes have on either of you if you want to further your education, or are in the process of doing that now?

What impact will conflicts on the role of education have on your children?

How will plans for further education affect your life together (e.g., time spent apart, economic pressures, having and/or raising children)?

If the relationship is new, what do you know about your partner's educational background? Have you verified it? (Sometimes people exaggerate their accomplishments to win favor.)

How do either of your attitudes toward education affect your attitudes toward work and family?

♥

19. EXPRESSING **EMOTIONAL** HONESTY

How successful are you each at reflecting on your own behavior and getting at the true feelings behind your actions?

Do you or your partner have trouble admitting to mistakes and blind spots? How much of this stems from a fear of rejection?

When one of you feels the other is not being emotionally honest, are you effective dealing with it as a couple?

How do you know what your partner is thinking or feeling about a problem or a concern?

If your partner isn't emotionally honest, how much is intentional? How much is a product of early childhood experience? Emotional problems? Intelligence? How upsetting is this to you?

How much emotional *dishonesty* in the relationship is a deliberate attempt to avoid closeness, strike out, hurt, embarrass, deny?

How much emotional *withholding* is a deliberate attempt to avoid pain, embarrassment, confrontation, negation, intimacy? How do you respond when one of you withdraws?

If either you or your partner is weak in the area of *verbal* expression, what other ways do you show emotional honesty/dishonesty (e.g., positive physical gestures, anger, defensiveness, violence, use of drugs/alcohol, withdrawal, outside involvements, workaholism, etc.)?

♥

20. ENERGY LEVEL ISSUES

Do you have a characteristic level of energy as a couple (e.g., always on the go, never get around to doing anything, like taking it easy)? How does this contribute to or detract from the relationship?

If there are differences in your levels of energy (e.g., hyperactive, never rests, always on the go, versus slow or lazy, tired a good deal of the time, needs a lot of quiet time), does it cause conflict? How?

What areas are affected positively and/or negatively by your differing or similar energy levels?

Is some flexibility or adjustment possible?

21. **FAMILY** BACKGROUND ISSUES

What do you know about your partner's family? What does your partner know about yours?

Are you familiar with each other's extended family background?

Have you compared your relationship with your parents' relationships, or those of siblings?

Are you unconsciously or consciously patterning your relationship on that of your parents? Is that good/bad for your relationship?

What are the differences and/or similarities between your partner's general family background and yours, (e.g., family size, education level, career level, style of child rearing, rural or city, etc.)? How do these similarities/differences affect your relationship?

What serious problems in your partner's or your family history might have a negative impact on your relationship (e.g., mental illness, drug use, genetic disorders or illness, etc.)? Have you shared these concerns? If not, why?

♥

22. EXPRESSING **FEELINGS**/HAVING FEELINGS

How capable are you each of recognizing your own feeling states? Each other's? Is your style of expressing feelings similar/different from your parent(s)?

How successful are each of you at expressing your feelings?

Which feelings are easiest/hardest for you (your partner) to own up to?

What feelings are easiest/hardest for you (your partner) to express?

Can you and your partner control your emotions and behavior and put feelings into words before acting/reacting negatively and destructively?

Do you have ways of expressing your feelings that drive your partner nuts? Vice versa? What are they?

How do you help or hinder each other in getting in touch with feelings?

If your partner can't acknowledge many feelings, how does this affect you? The relationship?

How much does your fear of rejection, ridicule, or anger inhibit how openly you express certain feelings?

♥

23. FERTILITY ISSUES

Do you agree on whether or not to have children? If you want children, do you agree on when to have them and on how many?

Are you clear with each other about your views on birth control and the issue of abortion?

Do your religious/ethical beliefs agree or disagree on fertility issues, pregnancy termination, birth control, adoption, etc.?

If you have agreed to raise children and are infertile, have you discussed other alternatives (e.g., adoption, artificial insemination, etc.)? Is there conflict here? Are you both willing to seek professional (medical and/or counseling) help?

If you are in a fertility program, how are you handling the stresses and strains? Have you discussed your feelings about being a childless couple vs. being parents together?

♥

24. ATTITUDE TOWARD **FOOD** AND EATING

Does food play an important role in your relationship (e.g., eating out, formal dinners at home, celebrations built around food, dieting together)?

Do you agree on when, where, and what to eat? Is it a significant problem?

Do you disagree over who is eating too much, not enough?

Are you both happy with the arrangement you have for who does the shopping, cooking, cleaning up after eating?

What bothers (pleases) you the most about your own and your partner's attitudes about food and eating?

If either of you has an eating disorder, have you talked openly about this? If not, why? If so, how are you each handling the problem?

Do you both enjoy the same kinds of foods?

♥

25. ATTITUDE TOWARD **FRIENDSHIP**

Have you met each other's friends? If not, why not? Does that suggest a hidden problem?

What do you know about each other's friendships? What do they say about the kind of person you are (your partner is)?

How well do you interact with each other's friends? How important is it to each of you that you like the other's friends and/or that they like you?

How influenced are you by your friends? How influenced do you think your partner is by his or her friends? Is it mostly positive or negative?

Is there a good balance between time spent with friends and with each other?

Do you agree on the importance of friends to each of you and to your relationship?

Do you have friends as a couple? Do you both like them? Are you equally interested in them?

Are your friends old or new or a combination of both?

Do you maintain friendships over a long period of time? Does your partner? Is this important to you?

Do your friends tend to be like you or do you have friends of various races, ages, sexes, and classes?

How much do you judge yourself (your partner) on the basis of how you each act with and treat your friends?

♥

26. HAVING FUN

Are you having fun together?

Do you know how to have fun together?

Do you agree on the importance of having fun together?

Do you have as much fun together as you used to? If not, what have you stopped doing together that was fun?

How do you celebrate together and pay homage to joyful events and accomplishments?

Are there occasions when taking time out for fun results in neglecting the basic problems and needs in the relationship?

Do either of you have trouble having fun?

Is either of you skilled at creating fun? Are you able to turn some jobs into fun to take the edge or boredom off the chore? If not, what possibilities are there for doing this?

Are there any games or hobbies you would like to play with your partner (e.g., join a book club, play cards, board games, or take up a sport) to increase the level of fun you have as a couple?

What adventures do you (or could you) plan together to break up the mundane routine?

How do each of you feel about taking time out once in a while to have a bit of frivolous fun and games?

♥

27. SETTING **GOALS**

How well or poorly do you discuss your goals and adapt to each other's needs?

What kinds of short-term and long-term goals do you set together?

What are your most important goals? Your partner's?

How closely do your individual goals mesh?

How open are you in talking about your goals, sharing your ongoing doubts, fears, hopes, and dreams?

Do you spend enough time setting mutual goals?

How well or poorly are you doing in setting goals for the relationship itself?

Is goal setting a collaborative process of joint decision making, consensus, and compromise?

How do differences in your goals or the style of setting them lead to conflict or affect your relationship?

If you are at different stages in your goal development (e.g., seeking independence, seeking interdependence in a relationship, developing a career, nest building, having children, wanting travel and adventure, wishing to settle down, etc.), how does this affect your relationship?

28. HABITS

Do either of you have any habits that could ruin the relationship if they aren't changed?

Are you able to discuss personal habits that you each find annoying? Is change possible?

Do some of your partner's habits, routines, rituals, or characteristics worry you because they might be signs of mental illness, obsessions, compulsions, or addictions?

Do you and/or your partner focus on annoying personal habits rather than deal with other more important problems in the relationship? As a way to avoid the bigger problems?

Is either of you in the habit of being too picky?

29. **HEALTH** ISSUES

If there are past, current, or potential health problems, how does this affect your relationship?

How open are you with each other about health problems?

Do you take good care of yourselves (e.g., exercise, diet, rest, check-ups, etc.)?

Are you supportive or critical about how your partner takes care of himself or herself?

How would you characterize your current health status? Your partner's?

Do either of you do things that jeopardize your health and trouble your partner?

If either of you has a physical handicap, how well or poorly do you deal with it as a couple?

If you became ill or handicapped, do you think your partner could and would cope with it lovingly? Would you cope lovingly with an incapacity or illness on your partner's side?

♥

30. HOBBIES AND OUTSIDE INTERESTS

Do you share any outside interests and hobbies? If not, and it's not okay, what can you do to change this situation?

Do either of your outside interests and hobbies cause conflict (e.g., too much time spent away pursuing the interest)?

Do either of your outside interests cause problems around the issues of ethics, trust, physical safety, or finances (e.g., time spent in bars, skydiving, gambling, etc.)?

How do your individual involvements in outside activities affect your ability to meet each other's needs and desires?

Do either of you feel it is important to develop more outside interests and hobbies to improve the quality of your lives?

♥

31. ATTITUDE TOWARD **HOME** AND HOME CARE

Do your individual attitudes and approaches toward housekeeping agree or disagree? If there are differences, how do they affect you and your relationship?

Do you each feel that housekeeping tasks are (should be) fairly distributed? Are you both willing to make changes?

Does having and caring for a home (apartment) symbolize the same things to you and your partner? If not, how does this affect the relationship?

If this is a new relationship, what can you learn from the appearance and care of your partner's home (apartment)?

Do you both keep your word about beginning or completing a task or is this a source of conflict?

Are you and your partner comfortable with each other's ways of going about household tasks? What are the problem areas?

Are you open to suggestion about how to do something differently in your house (apartment) without becoming defensive and angry?

♥

32. BEING **HONEST**

How do you agree/differ on the degree of honesty you expect in a relationship?

Have you ever caught your partner in a lie or been caught in one yourself? How has it affected your relationship?

What prevents you from being honest, forthcoming, candid about your needs, wants, likes and dislikes, priorities, and values?

Can you (your partner) be honest, admit mistakes about judgment or deeds, admit to negative feelings and behaviors? If not, why?

What would you like to know about your partner that he or she has not already told you?

If the relationship is new, do you know of anything that has happened currently or in your partner's past that is a red flag—i.e., that makes you doubt your partner's honesty, veracity, or integrity?

What do other people who know your partner better than you do say about your partner's honesty?

♥

33. HAVING A SENSE OF **HUMOR**

Do you find a lot to laugh about together?

How crucial is it for your partner to have a sense of humor?

Do your styles of humor match or complement each other? If not, how much does it matter to you?

How successful are you at laughing at yourselves and at your own foibles?

Do either of you use humor to cover up bad feelings, troubling situations, or serious problems that you should face head-on? Which ones?

When humor is used to make fun of each other's feelings or ideas or to minimize each other's concerns, or to belittle them, how does that affect your feelings for each other?

34. PERSONAL **HYGIENE** ISSUES

Do your individual standards of personal hygiene meet with consensus or conflict (e.g., teeth and body cleanliness, changing clothes, neatness and orderliness around the house)?

Can you talk openly about differences or are you embarrassed? Can you reach acceptable compromises?

If your standards do not agree, how do the differences cause problems?

Do you think that your or your partner's personal hygiene routines are adequate? If not, what can you do to improve them?

♥

35. **LEGAL** ISSUES

Are there past, present, or potential legal issues (divorce, civil suits, criminal action) that could greatly affect your relationship?

Have either of you ever been arrested for criminal behavior? If so, what were the charges (e.g., violence, robbery, fraud, misdemeanor, felony, etc.)? The circumstances? The age? The outcome? Is it out in the open?

Have either of you ever been involved in litigation? Civil, criminal? Currently? Is it out in the open?

Have either of you ever been sued? If so, for what, how often, and what was the outcome in each instance?

Do your views of the legal system mesh?

What is your partner's driving record (e.g., types of problems, charges, and frequency of problems, including accidents)?

If you or your partner have been divorced (or is currently involved in a divorce proceeding), how have you handled it (e.g., fair-minded, vindictive, obsessive, not sufficiently self-protective, overly legalistic)?

36. LISTENING

How well do you listen to expressions of feelings, worries, and triumphs from each other and from others?

How would you characterize your responses and your partner's (e.g., thoughtful, appropriate, critical, disapproving, argumentative, disinterested, distracted)?

When you listen do you confirm with your partner that you're hearing accurately?

Can you each listen long enough to hear the other's point of view?

Can you listen to criticism about yourself with an open mind?

How can you give criticism in a helpful way?

If listening is a problem, what steps can you take to improve the situation?

♥

37. EXPRESSING **LOVE**

How satisfactorily do you express feelings of love to your partner? To others (e.g., family, children, friends, and animals)? If not satisfactory, why?

Do you think your partner expresses his or her love for you adequately? If not, what prevents it? Are there steps you can both take to improve it?

Do you share expressions of love through gestures and tokens of affection?

How do you express and receive physical expressions of love (e.g., hugs, kisses, sex)?

What needs are or aren't met by the way your partner expresses his or her love?

♥

38. MARITAL STATUS ISSUES

How much do you know about your partner's marital status—past or present?

What have you shared with your partner about your marital status—past or present?

How much is your relationship affected by your or your partner's past or present marital status?

If you or your partner are divorced or separated, what do you think of how the breakup was explained? What themes, if any, emerge (e.g., blames others, blames self, takes responsibility for his or her part, feels victimized, etc.)?

What is your honest opinion of your partner's prior choice of a partner?

If you have differing attitudes toward marriage, how does this affect your relationship?

How do your partner's attitudes toward marriage meet or not meet your needs and expectations for the relationship?

♥

39. MENTAL HEALTH ISSUES

How do your individual attitudes about mental health issues and handling emotions, personal problems, and relationship problems mesh with each other?

If your attitudes differ, what effect is this having on the relationship?

How do you feel about seeking outside help in time of emotional crisis?

If you or your partner have had any serious psychiatric problems in the past (e.g., depression, psychotic break, suicide attempt), how much have you shared about it? What details haven't been discussed that should be?

If either of you is on medication or in treatment, how is it affecting your relationship?

Are there any serious mental health problems in your partner's family or in yours that could affect your relationship (e.g., current5s, congenital problems, chronic disabilities, etc.)? What steps are you taking to deal with them?

♥

40. HANDLING **MONEY**

Are you or your partner too impulsive, too reckless, too miserly when it comes to spending money? Does it threaten your relationship?

Are money decisions that affect the relationship reached by mutual consent?

How do you handle your financial obligations, responsibilities? How would you characterize your style? If your style differs from your partner's, does this cause conflict? How?

How does your partner's way of handling money affect your plans and needs, the future stability of your relationship?

Is there anything that you have noticed or heard about the way your partner handles money that causes you concern? Is this something you can discuss openly with your partner?

Are any areas of your partner's money handling still a mystery to you?

How does the way you handle money cause problems in other parts of your lives outside of the relationship? In other areas of your relationship?

What realistic plans do you have, backed by action, with regard to current and future financial needs or dreams as a couple?

How would you characterize your (your partner's) abilities to spend and to save? What are your feelings about both?

♥

41. MOOD AND EMOTIONAL ISSUES

Do you find your partner's moods easy or difficult to live with? Does he or she find it easy or difficult to live with yours?

Do you think that either of you lets your moods interfere with your judgment or consideration of the other?

Do you find your partner's moods generally appropriate and predictable?

How do you each handle negative moods (e.g., talk them out, act them out destructively, go for a walk to cool off, work on a hobby or a sport, take them out on others, get angry, take drugs, withdraw)?

Do your partner's moods ever frighten you? Are they a sign of deep-seated problems? What's your best and safest course of action?

How good or bad are you at picking up each other's moods?

Are you both open to exploring what triggers your moods?

Are you and your partner both open to accepting criticism, or are you (your partner) quick to be defensive and resentful, however well-meaning the remarks?

♥

42. ATTITUDE ABOUT **MORALITY**

Have you established valued standards of morality in your relationship that you value?

Have you felt the need to address your partner's lack of morality?

How do you agree/differ on morality? How does it affect you?

How do you each go about getting what you want (e.g., honestly, openly, deceptively, manipulatively, with hard work and concern for others)?

How opportunistic are you? Your partner?

Do you know of anybody your partner has knowingly hurt to achieve his or her own ends?

What do other people say about your partner's morality?

How does your partner feel and act if a friend deviates from the straight and narrow?

Have you or your partner ever stolen, cheated, or lied within or outside the relationship? If so, what were the circumstances (e.g., in business, personal life, wartime, etc.) and how often did it happen?

Do you think you and/or your partner have different standards and principles for different aspects of your lives?

How immoral would your partner have to be for you to terminate the relationship?

♥

43. EXPRESSING **NEEDS**

How do you get your needs met in the relationship? Are you satisfied? If not, why?

Do you and your partner agree on the role of the relationship in meeting each other's needs?

Is there enough trust and openness in the relationship for each of you to express your needs to each other?

Can you list your priority needs? Your partner's?

How do you communicate your needs? Do either of you have a problem expressing needs or understanding them?

Do either of you feel that expressing needs is a sign of weakness or inadequacy? How does this affect your relationship?

Are you aware of, and do you accept, gender differences in expressing needs and wants in your relationship and understand how these differences affect you?

♥

44. SHOWING **OPENNESS**

Are you each appropriately open and candid, or secretive and cryptic, tell too much too soon, beat around the bush about feelings, fears, concerns, and opinions?

How openly do you and your partner share your concerns and reveal what is on your minds?

How do you let each other know what is bothering you?

How do you express your triumphs and joys as well as your disappointments?

How successful are you at being open about the reasons for the feelings you have?

Are you comfortable letting your partner see your vulnerabilities, and vice versa?

What is your partner's reaction when you openly express your feelings, fears, doubts, etc.? Vice versa?

How openly do you share past, current, and future experiences, fears, concerns, and opinions?

What inhibits you from being as open as you would like to be? What do you think inhibits your partner? Are there underlying problems or issues?

♥

45. RELATIONSHIPS WITH **PARENTS** AND IN-LAWS

How does your involvement with each other's families affect your relationship?

Do you agree on how involved to be with each other's families?

Does your family or your partner's family cause conflict by placing expectations on you, your partner, or your relationship?

How do you feel about your own families? About each other's?

Can you accept each other's family?

Are you accepted by each other's family?

♥

46. ATTITUDE TOWARD **PAST RELATIONSHIPS** (PSYCHO/SOCIAL AND SEXUAL HISTORY)

What things disturb you most about your partner's past relationships? What about yours disturbs your partner?

How do your own or your partner's past relationships affect your feelings about making a commitment to this relationship?

Are there any patterns that you recognize in your partner's past relationships that remind you of your relationship with him or her?

How much do you talk about past relationships and what do you say?

What has your partner shared that raises a "red flag," i.e., makes you nervous or anxious?

Do you have to be careful about what you say?

If you or your partner are still caught up in a past relationship, how does it affect your relationship with each other? What are you doing to settle unresolved feelings?

What questions about your partner's past relationships would you like to have answered? How can you get those answers?

♥

47. CARING FOR/ABOUT **PETS** AND PLANTS

Do your attitudes toward care of pets and plants mesh? If you disagree, is there room for compromise?

Have you been able to establish any kind of shared responsibility toward your plants and pets?

What kinds of conflicts arise in your relationship because of your or your partner's pet? Is it dogs versus cats? Animals versus no animals? How far are you each willing to go to resolve these conflicts?

48. HAVING **PHYSICAL** SKILLS

If physical skills are lacking, or are present in abundance, how does this affect your relationship?

In what ways is having physical skills important to you? To your partner?

Do differences between your level of physical skills (e.g., fixing things, being coordinated, athletic, etc.) become a source of conflict, frustration, irritation?

Are there skills either of you need to learn or could teach each other that would help develop your physical adeptness and improve the relationship?

♥

49. BEING **POLITE**/CORDIAL

Do cordiality and politeness play a significant enough part in your relationship to suit each of you? In what ways?

Do you use the common everyday expressions of good manners with each other (e.g., please, excuse me, thank you, I'm sorry, etc.)?

Do either of you wish that the other were more mannerly, tactful, and courteous?

Have cordiality and politeness ever been able to smooth over a difficult situation in your relationship? If so, when and how did it help?

Are you polite and cordial to each other's friends, family, colleagues, or is this a problem?

♥

50. POLITICAL VIEWS

How would you characterize your (your partner's) political opinions, (e.g., left of center, center, right of center, revolutionary, liberal, conservative, uninvolved, only votes, couldn't care less)?

Do your political views and degree of political involvement agree or disagree? If they disagree, how much does it matter to you? To your partner?

Do you feel your partner's political opinions reflect his or her character and way of thinking? What pluses or minuses does this create for you?

Does one of you want to discuss politics more than the other?

Do you fight over political opinions?

51. PROBLEM-SOLVING STYLE, ATTITUDE, AND ABILITY

Are your problem-solving styles similar, contrasting, complementary, conflicting, utterly incompatible (e.g., must do it alone, open to discussion and other opinions, acts impulsively, can accept criticism, wants others to rigidly accept own solution, can act cooperately to solve a problem)?

Do you tend to solve problems alone or together? Is the decision affected by whether they're your problems, your partner's, or your problems together? How?

When you solve problems as a couple, does it bring you closer together or push you farther apart?

Does problem-solving together produce interesting conversations or serious fights?

When you put your heads together, do you ever come up with clever solutions to difficult problems?

When you solve a problem alone or together, is one or the other of you left feeling burned?

When either of you acts independently to solve a problem without consideration of its affect on the other, how does this affect your relationship?

How do you resolve power struggles?

What ground rules would help you in solving problems together?

♥

52. BEING **REASONABLE** AND FAIR

How does your (your partner's) ability or inability to be reasonable and play fairly affect your relationship?

Can you count on your partner to act in the interest of what's best for the relationship when push comes to shove?

Do you often end up feeling hurt because your partner has decided on an action that doesn't take your needs or wishes into account?

Do you take comfort in knowing that no matter how tough the negotiation and no matter how heated the difference of opinion, no matter how big the gap in understanding, your partner will never be moved to take advantage of you?

In what areas are you (your partner) most reasonable and fair in your dealings with each other? Least reasonable and fair?

Does your partner treat you better (or worse) than he or she treats others? Do you treat your partner better (or worse) than you treat others?

When your partner is unfair or unreasonable, do you have a satisfactory way to deal with it?

♥

53. BEING **RELIABLE**

How much can you rely on each other to keep your word and follow through on promises (e.g., to phone, keep appointments, carry out commitments, finish jobs, etc.)?

Do either of you have a history of making promises you couldn't or wouldn't keep?

Are you or your partner more/less reliable with each other than you are with other people? How do you feel about this? Does it create problems?

Are your partner's attitudes, behaviors, and feelings generally predictable and reliable even if you don't always like them?

What kind of feedback can you get (or have you gotten) from other people about your partner's reliability? How seriously are you taking what you learn?

♥

54. BEING **ROMANTIC**

Is romance an important part of your relationship? If not, do you wish it were?

What kind of romantic experiences do you and your partner share (e.g. flowers, time together for love and closeness, poems, quiet time together, go for walks, take vacations to romantic spots, take weekend getaways, have romantic dates, candlelit dinners, etc.)?

Has there been a change over time in the amount and quality of romance you share? More or less? Better or worse?

55. HAVING **SEX**

Is your sexual relationship as passionate, frequent, loving, sexy as you wish? Is it good enough?

If you disagree about the importance sex plays in your relationship, how do you deal with it?

If this is an old relationship, has the importance or the fun of sex diminished? Increased?

How open are you and your partner to discussing the nitty-gritty details of safe sex and your sexual relationship in general?

Are you comfortable or at odds about who takes responsibility for birth control and safe sex?

Did (will) you know your partner's HIV status before having sex? Have you discussed the AIDS threat if either of you is sexually active with other partners, or has been in the past?

How does using or not using safe sex methods or birth control affect your sex life?

What happens when you disagree about when or how to have sex? Can you and your partner each feel okay about saying no to having sex or to some sexual practice, and have it unconditionally respected? If not, why?

Do you talk openly about sexual needs, wishes, fantasies, and desires? If you think you should, but you don't, what stops you?

How often do either, or both, of you use having or not having sex to cover up or avoid problems? As a weapon?

Do you have problems and/or disagreements about extramarital or extra-relationship sexual encounters?

Do you know whether your partner used safe sex practices in past relationships? If your partner was or is sexually active outside of the relationship, do you know if he or she used (uses) safe sex practices? Did (do) you?

♥

56. **SEXISM** ISSUES

Do you each receive equal opportunity within your relationship?

Does your relationship support each other's striving for accomplishment, personal improvement?

Do you have fights about unfair, sexist treatment?

Are your financial benefits and the financial responsibilities shared reasonably and equitably?

Is the power shared in your relationship or does one person dominate?

Do either of you show prejudices about the opposite sex (e.g., make negative remarks, treat others of the opposite sex poorly, make disparaging jokes)?

Do either of you make gender distinctions when it comes to personal involvements? Business dealings?

Has sexual harassment ever played a role in either of your lives? In your relationship?

♥

57. HAVING **SOCIAL SKILLS**

Has behavior in social situations been a source of pride, anger, or indifference?

Does your partner have social skills that are up to your standards? Are yours up to your partner's standards?

What social skills do you feel are lacking in your partner? Which ones has your partner expressed as lacking in you?

If social skills are lacking on your part or your partner's, how does it affect your relationship?

Are there cultural or class differences that affect the differences in your social skills? How do these differences affect the relationship?

Are you each aware of your effect on other people's moods and needs? If not, what impact does that have on your relationship?

♥

58. BEING INVOLVED IN **SPORTS**

How does your and/or your partner's involvement and participation in sports affect the quality of your life together?

If you don't have the same level of involvement and interest in sports and physical activity, what conflicts ensue?

Is involvement in sports used to avoid problems or intimacy in your life together?

Can you participate in a sport or share an interest in watching or attending sports events together? If not, how much of a difference does it make to you?

Does your interest or your partner's interest and/or participation in sports conflict with the needs or expectations either of you has for the other?

♥

59. BEING **SUPPORTIVE**

Can you rely on each other to be supportive of your life plans and goals? If not, why?

Can you accept support and reassurance from each other? If not, how does it affect your relationship?

Are you there for each other during times of emotional stress? Times of joy and triumph? For the mundane upsets and concerns of everyday life?

Can you be supportive and sympathetic without having to "fix it" for the other?

When you're supportive, is it recognized as such? Is it appreciated?

What kind of support do you want from your partner? What kind of support do you think your partner wants from you? Have you talked about this?

♥

60. ISSUES OF **TASTE**

Are significant similarities in taste a positive aspect of your relationship?

How do differences in taste affect how you feel about each other?

What limits do these differences in taste impose on your relationship?

How important is it for you to like the same things?

In what areas do you share similar tastes? Is that pleasing? Share different tastes? Which differences bother you?

If you have different tastes do you try to impose your preferences on each other? What happens if and when you do?

How do you show tolerance/intolerance in regard to each other's taste differences?

Have your tastes become more or less similar over time?

♥

61. ATTITUDE TOWARD **TIME**

Do you have differing attitudes about issues that relate to time (e.g., being late/on time, missing/making deadlines, procrastinating/getting right down to things, coming in just under the wire, coming up with excuses)?

If you have differing attitudes toward time, what problems or conflicts does it create? How do you typically handle these conflicts?

How different are your needs for time alone and time together? Do they conflict?

How would you describe yourself and your partner in relation to time issues (e.g., compelled to stick to a rigid time schedule, everything has to be completely planned in advance, flexible about time, casual, concerned)?

In what way do differences in the time it takes for each of you to get things accomplished affect your relationship?

What impact do your attitudes toward time have on other issues—trust, reliability, honesty, support, problem-solving, etc.?

62. TRUSTING

Do you feel you can count on yourself and your partner to keep your word, follow through, tell the truth, etc.?

Has your partner betrayed you (e.g., had an affair, made fun of you in public, told others your secrets, misused your private property, hurt you physically, etc.)?

Do you have any reason whatsoever to mistrust your partner? Do you give your partner reason to mistrust you?

Can you trust your partner not to lie or to omit information? What kind of lie would you find most difficult to forgive?

Does your partner surprise you with new information or new behaviors that are disturbing?

Is there anything that you have lied about to your partner or omitted that he or she has the right to know about you?

If this is a new relationship, which are the areas that you know enough to be trusting in? What areas trouble you?

♥

63. WATCHING TV

Does TV time add to or take away from the quality of your relationship?

Do you have conflict or consensus over what and how much to watch?

Do you fight over who handles the remote control? Do you watch together or apart?

Does TV time interfere with, enhance, or not affect your sex life, your fun time, conversations, etc.?

Do either or both of you watch TV to avoid doing other things? What could you do instead?

Would your life together be better without TV?

♥

64. ATTITUDE TOWARD **VACATIONS**

Are vacations a source of joy or stress in your lives together?

Who plans vacations? You? Your partner? Both of you together? Is the way you plan satisfactory?

Do you fight about what kind of vacation to take, where to go, how to travel? Does one of you always get your way? How negative are the fights? Do you end up with good solutions?

Do you and your partner have fun on vacations?

If problems arise between you while you are away on vacation, does it spoil everything? Can you resolve the problems easily or do you wish you'd never left home? Are there often problems on vacation? What are they?

Have you resorted to separate vacations to avoid problems with the whole mess? Does it work out?

♥

65. ETHNIC/CULTURAL/SOCIAL/SPIRITUAL/RELIGIOUS **VALUES**

Do your ethnic/spiritual/religious convictions more or less agree with your partner's? If there are differences, how much of an issue is this for you?

How big a part does spirituality/religion play in your relationship? Is it a source of strength and satisfaction?

How would you characterize your (your partner's) spiritual/religious beliefs (e.g., traditional, new age, liberal, orthodox, conservative, fundamentalist, atheist, agnostic, secular humanism, no preference)?

Do you and your partner differ in involvement in organized religion? Does this cause problems between you, with your families, in the community?

If there are religious differences, is there any common ground for sharing spirituality (e.g., common love of nature, doing community service together, taking in a foster child)?

Are ethnic differences a source of joy and discovery in your relationship or a source of conflict and contention?

Is your involvement in each other's ethnic background satisfactory?

In what ways do your differing ethnic backgrounds affect other aspects of your relationship?

Do you each try to help the other understand your ethnic background and culture? Are you both open to learning more? Participating more?

Do you come from different social classes? Has this affected where and how you live, your choice of friends, relations with your families—positively, negatively?

66. ATTITUDE TOWARD **WORK** AND EARNING A LIVING

Do you and your partner agree or disagree about your attitudes toward work (e.g., works to live, lives to work, workaholic, works only to get by, loves work, hates work, out of work, avoids work whenever possible, perfectionist, sloppy)?

Does the work that either of you do serve as a means of avoiding contact in the relationship?

Do you respect what each other does for a living? If there's disrespect on either side, how does it affect your relationship?

Does your partner have a stable or troubling work history? How much do you know about your partner's work history? Have you verified what you've been told? (People have been known to lie about work to make themselves look better in new relationships.)

Do either of you connect job stability with commitment to the relationship?

If either of you has had many job changes or has not worked in a while, what are the accompanying circumstances (e.g., economic climate, inadequate schooling, fired, laid off, advancement, return to school)? Is this a source of conflict?

How will future work plans affect your relationship?

CHAPTER SIX

EXPANDING
YOUR LEARNING

TAKING STOCK

Now that you've delved more deeply into the issues that you selected in our Smartcard sort, this is your opportunity to sit back and evaluate the strengths you have going for you in your relationship by answering the following questions.

♥

THE POSITIVES

Are the characteristics you love and value most in a relationship the same positives you ranked highest with your Smartcard sort?

Are you valuing the positives in your relationship enough or have you been taking some of those positives for granted?

Are you demonstrating that value to your partner?

Can you do more to enhance those strengths within your relationship?

Are there some positives missing that you feel optimistic about bringing into the relationship?

Is the best in your relationship made up of positives you don't care much about?

♥

THE NEGATIVES

Now that you've thought about the positives, let's turn to the problem areas and negative aspects within your relationship.

Are the qualities you hate in a relationship the very ones you ranked most negative with your Smartcard sort?

How serious are the problems in your relationship?

Have you sincerely tried to resolve them with your partner?

Are you in the kind of relationship you want?

Is the worst in your relationship made up of negatives that don't really trouble you?

Should you break it off or get professional help in making it work?

♥

THE UNKNOWNS

Do you have a lot of questions you still need to get clarified?

Have you been avoiding exploring the unknowns? Has your partner?

Do you feel optimistic/pessimistic/scared about exploring these issues now?

THE DISCARDS

Do you still feel none of these issues plays a part in your relationship?

♥

MORE IDEAS FOR LAYING YOUR CARDS ON THE TABLE

The Smartcards are a very versatile and powerful tool for examining all sorts of intimate relationships and making eye-opening comparisons between them. Below, you will find other suggestions for ways to use the Smartcards to expand your knowledge of relationships. Using your own imagination, you'll be able to devise even more ways to use the Smartcards as you grow increasingly familiar with the process.

♥

COMPARISON SORTS

➙ Do a Smartcard sort for your *worst* past relationship and compare it to your present one.
   Are you repeating the same mistakes?
   Is your current relationship the more viable of the two?
   Are you exchanging old problems for new ones?
   Are you making progress?

➙ Do a Smartcard sort for your *best* past relationship and compare it to your present one.
   How does your present one stack up?
   Same features?
   Same flaws?
   Are you doing better? Worse?
   Are you settling for whatever you can get?

PARENT SORTS

➔ Do a Smartcard sort of your parents' and/or your partner's parents' relationship.

How similar is your relationship to theirs?

How many of their problems are you mirroring?

If you're going out of your way not to repeat their mistakes, is that causing you to be making some new ones of your own as a reaction?

♥

IDEAL SORTS

➔ Try selecting those Smartcards that suit your ideal relationship.

Use this as a reference point for your "real" relationships.

How close have you come to your ideal?

How realistic is your ideal?

What real issues don't stack up as compared to your ideal, and can these issues be improved?

♥

COUPLE SORTS

> **I must caution you to think carefully before you try putting your cards on the table together, as this comparison process can create a potentially explosive situation.**

You must feel confident of the ability of you and your partner to deal with differences before you do the Smartcard sort together, or before you even compare your results after doing them separately. Comparing Smartcard sorts highlights divisions and differences that can hurt and overwhelm one or both of you. If you suspect this might happen, I strongly advise you to do the Smartcards together in the presence of a professional psychotherapist.

→ Have your partner do a Smartcard sort on your relationship and compare his or her results to yours.

→ Do a Smartcard sort from what you think your partner's perspective would be. Then have your partner do a sort so you can see how close or far off you were. Your partner can do the same process in reverse.

How do your positives and negatives match up or contrast?

Do you rate your positives and negatives similarly?

Are there any surprises, new discoveries, disturbing revelations?

Assuming you have carefully considered my warning and decide to proceed, try these sorts.

On the positive side, whether you trust your relationship and do the Smartcards with your partner unsupervised, or do them along with a psychotherapist (which may be your safer bet), the face-to-face comparison process can produce many benefits:

→ Compensates for the undue advantage of the most articulate, emotional, and demanding partner.

→ Brings out issues that were otherwise hidden.

→ Makes you both consider a wide range of good points as well as the negatives.

→ Gets you away from the tendency to churn over the same few issues ad infinitum.

→ Gives you the opportunity to compare what you each value most and least so you can reflect on the ways in which you've been working at cross purposes.

→ Helps you pinpoint the reason for a vague sense that things are not going right.

→ Overcomes the differences in male vs. female communication styles by having you both sorting and focusing on the same wide range of issues.

→ Creates an even playing field upon which you each get the equal opportunity to question, discuss, and try to understand the other's cardsorts.

Mark and Charlotte are a couple who are having serious intimacy problems, but they both feel committed to making their marriage work. It's plain to see the problem areas as they do their Smartcard sorts together in my office. Even though they each select a fair number of positives, they're at odds about which issues belong in their positive stacks. Indeed, a number of Mark's positives end up as negatives in Charlotte's sort and vice versa. There's even a problem in the cards they agree on in terms of ranking. On top of Mark's positive stack is SETTING GOALS. Charlotte ranks that card at the bottom of her positives. She ranks BEING CONSIDERATE as the most positive aspect of their relationship. This card doesn't even make it to Mark's positive stack.

As for the negatives, here, too, Mark and Charlotte have serious disagreement. While they both recognize some of the same problems, they again rank them in very different orders. Number one for Charlotte is LISTENING. For Mark, HAVING SEX takes the top ranking. Is it any wonder that intimacy is lacking in this relationship?

Charlotte and Mark find it painful to compare their Smartcard sorts. They both feel anger, disappointment, and frustration. At least, they conclude, they can see why things have worked out so poorly for them. But as they begin exploring their cards, they recognize links between his negative view of their sexual relationship and her negative view of how poorly Mark listens to her. Charlotte believes that if Mark were more attentive and more interested in listening to what she had to say, she would feel more interested in having sex. As Charlotte explains to Mark, having sex is far more than a physical act for her. She needs to feel an emotional closeness before she can feel a physical closeness. This lack of emotional closeness is also reflected in her negative cards. Although this need is something Charlotte has tried to get across to Mark many times in the past, now he's seeing it in black and white!

Mark feels that his own sexual frustration has made him impatient with Charlotte and he grants that sometimes he tunes her out deliberately as payback. They both agree they have never tackled their problems or concerns with each other in a constructive way. Their willingness to do this now is a real breakthrough for them. They are finally ready to look at how these negatives affect their entire relationship together.

Once Charlotte and Mark explore their negatives in greater depth and gain more insight into what's going on in their relationship, as well as learn how their negatives and positives interface and intermingle, they're even less inclined to throw in the towel. There are some significant positives here and several negatives that they can agree to work on together. The Smartcard sort has given them insight into each other that they never had before. They both see this as a hopeful starting point.

Like Charlotte and Mark, other couples in my practice have found that using the Smartcards together, while painful and unsettling, has created opportunities for constructive, meaningful conversation. Some of the couples I've worked with have found doing the traditional sort too overwhelming or upsetting, and instead have adapted unique ways to use the Smartcards to address their issues and concerns, and enhance communication.

Earlier, I wrote about Barbara, who felt that, after eleven years, her marriage to Steven was falling apart. After each of them did the Smartcards separately in my office, they were able to use the Smartcards together in a novel way that kept the lines of communication open on a daily basis. Each evening they would select two or three Smartcards for discussion—sometimes issues one or both felt were positive, sometimes issues one or both felt were negative, and occasionally they would discuss a couple of cards they selected at random (these were sometimes the most illuminating).

As Barbara told me, "Dealing with just a few issues at a time really allows us to discuss them in great depth. And for the first time in ages, Steven isn't claiming he has nothing to talk about. He takes hold of one of those cards and he just starts to open up. We get into great discussions. Sometimes they get heated, but we stick with it until we've talked it out as much as we can. And we keep a couple of the *positives* on hand to remind us that there's a real balance here." Barbara adds, "We've learned more about each other and our relationship in these past few months than we learned in the past eleven years put together."

Another couple, Linda and Paul, use the Smartcards to help them focus on how one issue affects other aspects of their relationship. Linda sees Paul as very rigid. In the past, Linda held this up as a broad obstacle that affected their entire relationship. However, when I suggest she go through the Smartcards and pick out all the issues that are negatively affected by Paul's rigidity, Linda selects only certain cards: ISSUES IN HAVING OR RAISING CHILDREN, DECISION MAKING, WATCHING TV, ATTITUDE TOWARD TIME, and HANDLING MONEY. I then ask Linda to sort out the Smartcards again, this time picking issues in which Paul's rigidity might actually be a positive feature of their relationship. She gives both Paul and me a dubious look, but as she starts going through the Smartcards, she's surprised to discover that there really are several areas in which Paul's rigidity is a positive feature: SETTING GOALS, ATTITUDE TOWARD FOOD AND EATING, LEGAL ISSUES, ATTITUDE TOWARD WORK AND EARNING A LIVING, and HEALTH ISSUES. Linda concedes that in these areas, Paul's rigidity helps establish some needed and even beneficial structure and controls.

Linda and Paul both feel better having the problem area delimited and appreciate the balance they gain by acknowledging the positive effects of Paul's rigidity. Equally important to the two of them is what amounts to a major revelation that many very important aspects of their relationship are actually completely *unaffected* by Paul's rigidity. Now, instead of Linda tossing out a blanket accusation and feeling frustrated when she gets nowhere with Paul on this issue, they can focus on the specific areas where his rigidity is a significant problem.

You can use the same processes as the couples I've presented here to keep the lines of communication open and energized in your own relationships, and to highlight how a particular personal characteristic or troubling issue affects (positively and negatively) certain areas of your relationship and not others.

♥

MAXIMIZE THE VALUE OF THE SMARTCARDS

Putting your Smartcards on the table provides a detailed map to guide you and your partner on your interpersonal travels together, allowing you to occupy the same space, and giving you both permission to openly and honestly look your relationship square in the eye. How well you cover the terrain is as important, however, as traveling through it. Moving into uncharted waters offers many new discoveries but also has its risks, dangers, and potential disasters. To best weather those storms and maximize the benefits of the Smartcards you'll need to learn the most powerful relationship survival ideas and techniques.

In the chapters that follow you'll find a map of a different sort—a global view that includes the structure of a good relationship, the behaviors that are necessary to keep a relationship healthy and thriving, an exposé of the myths and illusions that threaten your chances of achieving lasting love and commitment, the fears you have that keep you from getting close, and the golden rules for traveling together in style.

PART TWO
THE NATURE OF LOVE RELATIONSHIPS AND INTIMACY

CHAPTER SEVEN
FOUR MYTHS OF ROMANTIC LOVE

What is this thing called romance? All too often we imbue the romantic state of mind, or heart as it were, with all kinds of magical, mystical properties. When we're romantically in love, we feel convinced we've finally found that one person who truly cares for us, who will never disappoint us, never fail us, never leave us. At least while it lasts, we get lulled into feeling safe, secure, and on top of the world.

When we buy into romantic love as the be-all and end-all of our intimate relationships instead of merely the starting point, we are buying into all the myths that are attached to it. In the end, we are distraught to discover that what we've bought is ephemeral at best, heartrendingly painful and destructive at worst.

♥

MYTH #1:
THERE IS ONE GREAT AND ENDURING PASSION IN OUR LIVES

This myth of romantic love, the idea that we shall each find one great and lasting love in our lives, is very powerful and very destructive. As

143

so many of my patients have learned through experience and suffering, romantic love does not often endure. It cannot be indefinitely sustained on its own. Sooner or later, you fall *out* of love. With that fall goes the perfect acceptance and understanding you naively thought was eternally yours. Your dream lover turns into a real person, sometimes a stranger, sometimes a veritable monster. And, all too often, you can no longer even imagine what it was you saw in him or her in the first place.

In college, Nicole fell in love with Oscar, a popular athlete. He was her Prince Charming. They got engaged in their senior year and married right after graduation. Everyone, including the newlyweds themselves, saw them as the picture-perfect couple. "Oscar was the man of my dreams. I'd dated lots of guys, but none of them compared to Oscar. It was like I'd been waiting all my life for only him to come along. By the time he asked me out, I knew he was the one. It was magic. I could hardly breathe during our first date. We made love that night. I'd never, ever gone to bed with a guy on a first date. I was really pretty prudish. I'd only slept with a couple of other men. But with Oscar—well, we were both on fire. It was such a powerful force. Like nothing either of us had ever experienced before. And I honestly believed I could never, ever experience it again with any other man."

Nicole still clings to this myth that Oscar is the great love of her life even though, ten years later, she admits that her marriage is an unmitigated disaster. Oscar has had several affairs. Once, a few years back, he actually left her for another woman. But when he showed up at the front door a couple of weeks later, Nicole took him back. Six months later, she discovered he was having an affair with a neighbor.

Nicole has often thought about leaving Oscar, but she's convinced, for all the pain he's caused her, that he's the only man she can ever truly love. So what choice does she really have? And she keeps rationalizing to herself that for all the heartache, there's "something special" that binds them together.

The Smartcard sort gives Nicole the opportunity to find out what that indescribable, nebulous "something" is. She takes the Smartcards in hand and I can see her inner struggle as she grapples with each of the issues. She wavers in her placement of many of the cards. Is this a feature of her relationship? Is this a plus? Do they have this going for them? When Nicole has finally finished putting her cards on the table, it's a sad, but eye-opening, sort. There are almost no cards in Nicole's positive stack, and the few that she deems positives are not ones, she admits, that add much of consequence to their relationship.

"There's nothing here," she says with bewilderment. "What have I been clinging to all these years? *Who* have I been clinging to?"

Sadly, she's been clinging to a mythological man from a mythological tale, a false vision that actually promotes the antithesis of genuine intimacy. Don't you be fooled by the myth—genuine intimacy requires not merely emotionally charged passion, but knowledge, understanding, and a commitment to working together to create the valued quality in the relationship.

♥

MYTH #2:
LOVE CONQUERS ALL

You'd think that the dismal national divorce statistics would be enough to dispel this myth. But, diabolically, the widespread belief that love conquers all leads to thinking there's nothing you need learn to help yourself, and this misconception in turn leads marriages down the myth-strewn road to failure. Remember the Beatles singing, "All you need is love"? Fat chance! The specious belief that love conquers all fills you with false hope and leaves you planless, resourceless, and powerless to deal with all the inevitable problems of long-term intimate love. In the end you're left high and dry with bad feelings of betrayal.

Kathleen married Alan after a whirlwind courtship. She was convinced he would make an ideal husband. "He was so romantic, so charismatic. He was as crazy about me as I was about him. We thought we had it made; that no matter what happened, we had our love." Three years later, Kathleen sits in my office and stares at me in despair. "I don't know what happened. I thought Alan really loved me. I know I loved him, but now I don't know what I feel about him. Nothing's the way I thought it would be—the way it was supposed to be." She wears a lost, pained expression. "Was it all an illusion?"

Sad to say, the answer to Kathleen's question is a most emphatic "yes." Like so many of us, Kathleen and Alan bought heavily into the love-conquers-all myth. When problems began to crop up in their marriage, each of them expected that because they loved each other their problems would work themselves out. They bought the myth and got all the magical thinking that comes with it as a demonic bonus prize.

"We counted on some outside force to take care of things rather than on the two of us having to figure out solutions to our problems." Before Kathleen and Alan can even get to the problem-solving stage they will first have to understand what those problems are, how the two of them contribute to the creation and maintenance of the problems, and which problems need to be tackled with the most expediency.

Kathleen puts her Smartcards on the table and gets her first glimpse of the true complexity of a long-term relationship. She sees that neither she nor Alan ever created a foundation of shared knowledge, understanding, and interests as an underpinning to the romantic love they initially felt for each other. Instead of romance being a starting point from which to build something solid, they built their house of straw and the first wind that came along blew it right down. All either of them knew how to do was try to put another straw house up, and then another gust of wind came along...

♥

MYTH #3:
LOVE WILL CHANGE MY PARTNER

Like Dorothy in *The Wizard of Oz,* if you believe in this myth, you believe you can lead men (or women) of tin and straw to overcome their awe of witches and wizards, take control of their lives, and become truly human—in the image you have already created in your mind. You cling to the belief that if there are faults in your lover, through your love, you'll have the power to eliminate them. Unfortunately, love doesn't grant you any such power, and, more often than not, your partner's faults long outlast the romance.

Arlene fell madly in love with Ethan. But she makes it clear that she was never blind to his faults. She prides herself on her perceptiveness. "I never wore rose-colored glasses when I looked at Ethan. I knew just what I was getting into when I got involved with him. He could be very selfish and moody. And forget being reliable. The thing was, Ethan knew right from the start that these things bothered me. I was very up-front about that. And he never said anything to me like 'Hey, that's the way I am. Take it or leave it.' So I thought these were things he wanted to change and that, because he loved me so much, he'd really do something about them." Arlene honestly thought that the power of their mutual love would make him change for the better. When this didn't happen, Arlene drew the conclusion that Ethan just didn't love her enough. Instead of realizing that it was her belief in a destructive myth that had failed her, she ended up blaming Ethan for letting her down.

♥

MYTH #4:
ROMANTIC LOVE LASTS FOREVER

At the core of the myth of romantic love is the simplistic and heartfelt belief that your love will last forever. That belief is wholly based on your faith in romance—a faith that will betray you. The simple truth is that romantic feelings cannot last indefinitely in their original form or original intensity.

Sooner or later the time will come when your faith will fail you. Typically, you try to cling in desperation to your faith even as you question it. But you start to slip. Sometimes you "fall." Think of the word "fall," as in "falling" in love and "falling" out of love. It's as if the process occurs by *accident*—like stumbling over a log you didn't realize was blocking your path. Since romantic love is based on nothing more than the *accident* that began it, you can easily fall out of love.

When you "fall" out of romantic love, your faith having failed you, all too often you feel as if there's nothing left in that relationship. And tragically, for many there *is* nothing left—no foundation based on the real qualities that go into making up a loving, long-lasting, intimate relationship.

Inevitably the rosy hue fades, and those of you who live by this myth of eternal romantic love have nothing to replace it with, nothing substantial that can help you rekindle the original passion and excitement. You are left in deep pain, without any of the qualities in the relationship that can help you fall back in love with the same partner over and over again.

♥

WHY YOU CLING TO THE MYTHS

When you are "in love" you purposely avoid looking too closely or too deeply at your immediate relationship for fear of diminishing your feelings of elation and excitement. You avoid thinking much beyond dreamy fantasies of how great the person is—"He/she looks terrific. He's/she's fun. I love the way he/she dresses. And he's/she's a fabulous lover." Could this possibly be the stuff of a successful long-term relationship? Why would you want to kid yourselves so?

Because self-deceit is the natural state of the beast. In the throes of romantic love you are prepared to believe anything that maintains your good feelings. Nothing your partner says, nothing strange or worrisome you hear about your partner, makes the slightest dent in your blind enthusiasm. And a lifetime of living in a society that supports and nourishes the myths of romantic love through novels, films, even TV and advertising makes it all the harder to question and examine your "romantic high."

Further, that uplifting feeling, that rosy glow of romantic love, is more valued than ever in relatively depressed economic and psychological times. You have so much to worry about that being involved in a romance feels like just the kind of lift you need. What could be better? Being in love makes you feel great and it doesn't cost anything. Romantic love creates the illusion that all your woes are dispelled. Or so you think.

In truth, what happens is that you find yourself enveloped in a downward spiral. Instead of taking away your woes, unmitigated romantic love has the wicked power to reduce you to a state of exquisite suffering.

♥

WHEN THE MYTHS FAIL US

When you discover that romantic love does not cure all the ills within your relationship, or make your partner change as you fantasized, like Arlene you feel angry, cheated, and confused. And, nonsensically, as soon as you can get yourself back in gear, what do you do but set off once again on the quest for *true* romantic love. This time you're sure you'll get it right.

So you *fall in love again* with someone new. But romantic love, by its very nature, clouds your ability to rationally determine whether this new person you've fallen in love with is any better suited for you than your last love. Possibly you've hit pay dirt, but as I've shown in some of my earlier examples, you are rarely in a position to know early on whether this relationship could be viable over the long haul. Most people in an intimate love relationship, whether it's old or new, don't have the tools to evaluate the nature of the relationship itself or make any judgment calls about its viability.

♥

DON'T THROW OUT THE BABY WITH THE BATHWATER

There is nothing wrong with romantic love, only with the myths that tell you that you don't need to go beyond your feelings. You have to be careful not to allow your highly charged emotions to keep you from also having as realistic and broad a view of your relationship as possible. If you eschew the myths of romantic love and maintain a commitment to working on the quality of the relationship right from the beginning, you have the opportunity to add substance to your emotions, and provide a solid foundation upon which to build.

My point is not to discredit the joyful experience of romantic love or dismiss it as inconsequential. Being madly, wildly in love is exhilarating and exciting. Enjoy it. *For what it's worth*. If you're looking for a *good and lasting investment*, it will more than pay off in the end to examine your relationship head-on with the Smartcard sort, exploring the positives, negatives, and, very likely, the many issues you have yet to learn about in your romantic relationship. In my experience with patients, doing the Smartcards at the height of your romance can either save you a lot of unnecessary heartache by exposing the short-term prospects for the relationship or point the way toward adding substance to the froth of romance by highlighting productive issues to explore together.

Our Smartcard sort allows you, when you are in the throes of romantic love, to advance your burgeoning relationship by adding knowledge, understanding, and an opportunity for meaningful communication which actually sets the stage for falling back in love once the initial romance starts to tarnish. The Smartcard sort is a process and technique that can renew your faith in the relationship, only this time you can back your faith up with something tangible and concrete. In this way you create something consequential to fall back on when the bloom of passion has begun to fade. When you tend to the issues in your relationship beyond the infatuated feeling, you fall out of love all the same, but not into nothingness. Rather, you land in an active, ongoing constructive relationship.

CHAPTER EIGHT
THE TRUTH ABOUT INTIMACY

By the end of the seventies, the divorce rate had reached an all-time high, and it became painfully clear that romantic love alone was not succeeding as a basis for successful long-term relationships. The myths of romantic love began to share the stage with the new panacea of intimacy. The overselling of intimacy hit full stride in the high-flying eighties. It was the fast-food solution to relationship woes. Supposedly easy to get, intimacy was pushed as the feel-good cure-all for increasingly alienated couples. In the movie *Broadcast News,* Holly Hunter explains the notion to her love interest, William Hurt, on their first date, "It's that great feeling that you don't want to hold anything back. You know. Intimacy." But intimacy is not *feeling* open on occasion; intimacy is the hard-earned product of taking the time to *be* open to each other over a period of years.

♥

THE ROAD TO INTIMACY

It's heartbreakingly misleading to con people into believing there's an easy road to intimacy. Intimacy develops slowly out of a deep understanding of each other, an awareness of the problems within your relationship, an ability to work together on those problems, an appreciation of the features of your relationship, and the willingness and the daring to explore those uncharted territories together.

The overselling of a quick route to intimacy is a cruel hoax twice over. First, intimacy can't actually be readily achieved. It takes tremendous time and effort, which most couples can't supply. Second, and cruelest of all, if they ever did get to the nirvana of high intimacy, many would find out that it wasn't the solution to their relationship problems at all, but the source of even more problems caused by their perfectly normal discomfort with an overabundance of interdependency.

There is, however, a kernel of a very good idea in the intimacy movement which got lost in all the fervor, and that is that most couples could benefit significantly from controlled doses of intimacy in selected areas of their life. It is still a fairly high art to master and it still takes a significant amount of your time to practice it, but these controlled and selective doses of intimacy which I call *intentional intimacy* is a realistic goal that can be achieved through your use of the Smartcards and the ideas in the Loving Smart program.

If your relationship is based on romantic love, the Loving Smart approach to intimacy has two very powerful advantages. One: It provides you with a cushion of significant caring involvement for the times when you fall out of your romantic phase. Two: It provides opportunities for you to have the kind of accepting openness that has the power to rekindle the flame of romantic love, like a spark jumping an electrical gap when two live wires are brought close enough together.

A careful examination of your Smartcard sort for your love relationship may reveal that you have more areas of intimacy to start with than you might have expected. Terri and Dave are a successful career couple who have been married for four years. Terri describes herself as a "touchy-feely kind of person," whereas she describes Dave as "very self-contained." With despair she says, "He never likes to talk about his feelings and sometimes he actually looks pained when I talk about mine."

At first, when Terri does the Smartcard sort, she begins by pulling out only the negatives. These are the issues Dave refuses to discuss or ones in which they have sharp differences of opinion.

Terri attacks the remaining cards by first discarding the issues that she doesn't feel are important in the relationship. There aren't many. Terri feels most of the issues are pertinent. She's still left with about twenty-five Smartcards. A number of them get laid down on the unknown stack. "If Dave and I were closer," she says morosely, "there would hardly be a card on this stack."

What Terri's left with in her hand are the Smartcards that by process of elimination, she deems "positive." For all Terri's claim to wanting more closeness with Dave, she initially makes light of the dozen Smartcards that fall into the positive stack. Only after she starts ordering them and elaborating on their significance does she begin to gain an appreciation of these features of her relationship—such items as ETHNIC/CULTURAL/SOCIAL/SPIRITUAL/RELIGIOUS VALUES, TRUSTING, SETTING GOALS, HAVING SOCIAL SKILLS, HAVING A SENSE OF HUMOR, DECISION MAKING, and ATTITUDE ABOUT MORALITY.

In reviewing the positive features in her relationship with Dave, Terri acknowledges that all of these issues are very important to her. She's surprised and pleased to see how much real substance and value there is in these cards. There are other areas that she wishes were also positive features in the relationship, but by gaining a better appreciation of what she and Dave have going for them, she sees that these other areas needn't take center stage. Terri realizes that she's been so busy focusing on what's missing in the relationship that she hasn't given enough credit to what's actually there. Her renewed confidence in the relationship is communicated to Dave.

It's important to make the point here that intimacy is relative. Having a number of positive features in your relationship doesn't necessarily mean you have an *intimate* relationship. The positive features must hold significant value for you and enhance a true feeling of closeness between you and your partner. And that intimacy has to be weighed against your negatives. The negatives can detract considerably from your positives, seriously jeopardizing the degree of intimacy you've achieved. On the other hand, working together on those negatives and resolving them to any degree can be one of the most powerful methods for enhancing intimacy between you. You come through a battle, or even a war, together. Not only have you survived, but you've shared an incredible experience and gained a deeper understanding of each other along the way.

In Terri's case, she does feel that her positives reflect a significant level of intimacy that she shares with Dave. Although she would still like them to be more intimate, her mind-set is different now. As is Dave's. They're both more open to working constructively on some of the negatives. "Who knows?" Terri reflects. "Next time I do the sort, I may be shifting some of those cards from my negatives over to my positives stack.'' And if those positives hold enough meaning for her, they will further enhance her intimate relationship with Dave.

♥

THERE IS NO ONE TYPE OR AMOUNT OF INTIMACY THAT'S RIGHT FOR EVERYONE

The Smartcards give you the opportunity to get a lot more intimate with your partner. That doesn't mean it's always in your or your partner's best interest, or in the interest of the relationship itself, to jump right in on every issue and concern in an effort to get closer. You may get too close for comfort and end up growing closer and closer apart.

When you do your Smartcard sort, be careful to distinguish between the issues that truly concern you and those you think *should* concern you. Trying to fit your own intimate relationship to a standard set by others is a sure road to frustration and disappointment and can ultimately lead to a needless sense of failure.

Joyce and John, for instance, get along reasonably well. They own their own sporting goods shop and spend a great deal of time together, but they rarely discuss personal feelings. Most of the time they talk about the business, money matters, and their three children. Joyce, however, frequently compares her relationship with her husband, John, to that of her younger sister Liz's relationship to her husband, Greg. In the comparison, John usually comes up wanting. "Liz can tell Greg anything," Joyce says. "And Greg's the kind of man who can cry at a romantic movie and not be embarrassed.'' Greg is gregarious and emotional and loves to talk, all qualities Joyce finds lacking in John. She interprets this as meaning that she and John are not as intimate as they *should* be. It doesn't help matters that Liz reinforces her sister's disappointments. "Liz feels sorry for me. She's always telling me that I have to confront John more, get him to open up, demand that he show his feelings more.'' The implication is that Joyce and John do not have an intimate relationship because John is unable to meet her demands.

These disappointments show up in Joyce's Smartcard sort. As John examines the top cards in his wife's negative stack—SHOWING OPEN-NESS, HAVING CONVERSATIONS, EXPRESSING NEEDS, ARGUING AND FIGHTING, EXPRESSING FEELINGS/HAVING FEELINGS—he comments wearily, "The cards are stacked against me."

John's right. Joyce has stacked the Smartcards against him, using the problem areas that fit into her expectation of what defines intimacy as proof that their relationship is seriously lacking. Yet, when Joyce finally turns to her positives, ranking them and delving more deeply into how important these issues are in her marriage, she sees that she and John actually do share a fairly meaningful level of intimacy based on shared interests and agreements on important issues, such as HANDLING MONEY, ISSUES IN HAVING OR RAISING CHILDREN, HAVING SEX, HANDLING CRISES.

Returning to her negatives, I ask Joyce to select those issues that don't necessarily require John to "be more open and expressive." She selects HAVING FUN, HABITS, WATCHING TV, BEING ROMANTIC. Looking at these cards, John stops feeling on the defensive. These are areas he, too, acknowledges could be improved. He feels optimistic about working together with Joyce on these issues. The pressure is lifted. Both agree that making improvements in these areas would enhance their relationship and serve to make them feel closer, feel more intimate. It isn't that Joyce doesn't wish that John would be more open and expressive, but she no longer uses that trait as the only yardstick of intimacy in their relationship.

CHAPTER NINE

THE ARCHITECTURE OF GOOD RELATIONSHIPS

Not only is romantic love alone not enough to create a happy, long-term love relationship—intimacy isn't either. But artfully combine the two within a solidly structured relationship and you're talking turkey.

When I tell patients that relationships have an actual form and structure, they are, almost to the last one, astonished at such a revelation. "Form? Structure? Like a house?"

Yes, like a house. A building is a good analogy for the relationship structure. Start with the supporting beams or *pillars of a good relationship,* as I call them. Without these crucial pillars, the house will ultimately tumble, all the wood, shingles, bricks, whatever, crashing to the ground. Rubble. In much the same way, without establishing the *supporting beams* in a relationship, the crash will be just as inevitable, the rubble perhaps even more devastating.

There are four crucial pillars that must be in place in order for your relationship to have a good shot at success. And like the pillars of a house, they must all be in sound condition. If one or more pillars is badly damaged, the pressure on the remaining pillars increases and with it the potential of the roof caving in.

Another useful notion that the pillar image conveys is that the structure may be sound without the building being aesthetically pleasing. It's the same way with intimate relationships. You may achieve effective pairing—the making of a stable, solid, working relationship—without actually being thrilled with the entire design. This was certainly the case for many of the people I used as examples throughout the book.

Before I explain the pillars in detail, I want to make the point that, like houses, it's what goes inside of relationships as well as what holds them up that determines how much they mean to you. Even if your house has problems, there are many options to consider before gutting it and starting all over from scratch. A little straightening up, a bit of remodeling, some expansion, even accepting some of its limitations can make what seemed to be a hopeless building have exciting possibilities.

The stronger and more substantial the pillars, the more pressures they can withstand. Just like the house we build, the relationship we construct must be solid enough so that we can struggle through certain issues, have our disagreements, argue, and get a little sloppy, even dysfunctional at times, trusting to those pillars to hold up even under stress and duress.

In building a relationship, unlike a house, while all the pillars have to be substantial and solidly in place, they do not have to be of equal strength. This is because the pressure points in a relationship exert variable weight on each of these four pillars.

My discussion of the four pillars of effective long-term intimate relationships, begins with the one that bears the *least* heavy load and progresses to the others in increasingly weight-bearing importance.

♥

SOME GOOD SEX

This is the *least* important of the four essential pillars? Yes. It's amazing how far couples can go without very much decent sexual interaction. Sex is funny stuff. People think about it a lot, many think about sex incessantly, but most people don't have to do it a lot. Some individuals can achieve personal well-being without ever engaging in a sexual relationship. But that's a great rarity in couples. Almost all intimate couples pay the price when the passion quota drops critically low.

The funny stuff of sex affects relationships in two ways. One, when the frequency and intensity of the sexual relationship dips below what a particular couple needs, the vigor, flexibility, and loving potential of the union are all put in jeopardy. In the midst of the many stresses and strains of a couple's life, the exclusive, passionate sexual experience provides a primitive resealing of the relationship deal. After all, it's no accident that marriage itself is customarily sealed with sex on the wedding night. The spirit of that act needs to permeate the future relationship. Its repetition functions as an act of renewal. Sex is one of the simplest ways to give each other the good feeling that goes with the idea, *I'm getting something out of this relationship that's worth the trouble of being in it.*

Two, some good sex is a hedge against the danger of infidelity. *Good* sex goes with words like passionate, exciting, expressive, loving, exhilarating, intense, thrilling, powerful. The rule of thumb is that a couple needs to have at least *enough* good sex so that the partners can resist the temptation to go outside the relationship to satisfy their needs. At the very least, sex must be frequent enough and satisfying enough with your partner so that when temptation rears its come-hither head you're able to fight the lure off by remembering that you already have it pretty good.

Infidelity and happiness in committed love relationships are antithetical. I know of no case where infidelity has not caused very stressful and negative effects. The person who is engaging in the infidelity may rationalize sex outside his/her relationship quite readily, but he or she is rarely exempt from feelings of guilt. And it's even rarer to encounter the partner who does not inevitably feel hurt, humiliated, rejected, jealous, and enraged at learning of his or her partner's extracurricular sexual activity. By ignoring the pillar of some good sex, seeking it outside the intimate relationship becomes all too tempting, and happens all too frequently. The pillar, possibly poorly constructed in the first place, with repairs and adaptations ignored, starts to crumble, adding a great burden to the other three pillars.

Some and *good*—as in *some good sex*—are both relative terms. What's a lot of sex for one couple may be a serious lack of sex for another. What's good for one couple may be mediocre for another. The problem gets stickier when your sex drive differs sharply from your partner's, or your definitions of what's good are at odds.

Each couple must determine for themselves the amount and kind of sex they desire. If sex is infrequent enough or has fallen into a dreary, "time to do it" routine, the temptation for infidelity rises proportionately. Take Brad, who's off on a business trip that's stretching into the second week. A totally appealing single woman sales rep he's spent the day hopping in and out of the car with, and leaning over hot product samples with, flat out propositions him. "We're both tense from all this hard work, and we both could badly use some relaxation," she says. "It sure would be tension reducing," she quips seductively, moving in effectively to close the deal. Brad knows that this is a bad idea, but it's a very tempting one. He can summon up inner resolve if he can say to himself, "It's not like I never have any good sex. Nope, there's not enough to gain here compared to the risk." But Brad's going to have a much harder time saying no if he starts thinking "If I pass this up I'm going to my grave without ever having *any* hot sex." With that kind of motivation the disastrous transition from temptation to action may well seem worth the risk. Lust and self-pity are an incredibly powerful motivating combination, in this case combining to seriously threaten one of the most important aspects of any couple's life, the sanctity of their primary love relationship.

When HAVING SEX is defined as an issue that needs work, this is an opportunity to restructure the *some good sex* pillar. Let's return to my example of Mark and Charlotte, who were experiencing serious marital difficulties. Mark places HAVING SEX as the number-one issue on his negatives. Initially, Charlotte is very defensive. "Mark wouldn't be satisfied unless we had sex every night of the week." Mark counters, "Every night? Lets try once a week. Once a month!" The arguing escalates—a series of verbal punches and counterpunches, each jab aimed not at examining and facing the problem together, but at humiliating and disabling each other. This form of communication seems to be Mark's and Charlotte's style whenever it comes to grappling with issues affecting the relationship—big issues, small issues, it doesn't seem to matter. In this, they are remarkably and nonconstructively egalitarian. Indeed, they often toss other issues of concern haphazardly into the ring.

It is certainly true that one problem issue can lead to problems in other areas, but it's important, in order to be constructive, to carefully define the areas affected instead of tossing in everything but or including the kitchen sink.

Rather than engage in refereeing the fight between Mark and Charlotte, I ask both of them to go through their cards again and select those issues directly affected, either negatively or positively, by the issue of HAVING SEX. This stops the argument cold and provides the feuding pair with a concrete task, one that also requires considerable reflection.

They even manage a little smile when they notice they've each put ATTITUDE TOWARD VACATIONS on the top of their positive stacks. Both agree that, on vacation, sex is more frequent and more exciting. Charlotte and Mark have some good sex at least when they're vacationing. Unfortunately, they haven't taken a vacation in close to two years.

Mark's top negatives that are affected by his dissatisfaction with his sex life are ATTITUDE ABOUT MORALITY, USING/ABUSING DRUGS AND ALCOHOL, BEING AFFECTIONATE, and BEING REASONABLE AND FAIR. Mark fantasizes about having an affair even though he admits that the mere fantasy engenders feelings both of guilt and failure. He also attributes an occasional bout of too much drinking to sexual frustration. "If we're at a party and having a good time, but I know we aren't going to have sex when we get home, I drink enough so that I'll pretty much pass out as soon as my head hits the pillow." Mark says that he feels less affectionate toward Charlotte because of their infrequent sexual involvement and sees Charlotte's lack of interest in sex as a sign of her being unaffectionate. Lastly, Mark admits that his anger and frustration about sex affect BEING ROMANTIC, HAVING A SENSE OF HUMOR, even BEING POLITE/CORDIAL.

Charlotte's Smartcard sort over the issue of HAVING SEX is also telling. For one thing, she is able to see that it's her problem as well as Mark's. "If it's a big enough problem for him then it becomes my problem as well. Certainly, if he ended up having an affair, it would be a hell of a problem for both of us. It would probably mean the end of our marriage."

Charlotte explores her own Smartcard sort. Like Mark, she'd never realized how their sex life affected other aspects of their life together. She agrees that Mark's discontent over their sex life has a direct bearing on how much affection she expresses to Mark. "That's because if I'm affectionate I'm afraid he's going to always think I want sex. Sometimes I'd just like us to be affectionate, cuddle and snuggle and not have sex." Mark says some more cuddling and snuggling even without sex would go a long way toward his feeling closer with Charlotte.

Of special importance to both of them is Charlotte's selection of EXPRESSING NEEDS as a negative. "I've always been too embarrassed about telling Mark things I might like when we're making love. And I'm afraid he'll take it as an insult—like he isn't a good enough lover." She is surprised when Mark tells her he's not interested in being Don Juan, nor is he a mind reader. He'd love to know what she'd like. He even blushes, admitting he finds the prospect very erotic.

Mark and Charlotte recognized that they needed the help of a good "contractor," i.e., professional therapist, to help them rebuild the pillars of their relationship. Don't let shyness or feelings of shame keep you from getting the kind of help you need. If the level of *some good sex* cannot be reached after you've worked together to understand the problem fully, then I strongly recommend an evaluation, and perhaps treatment, from a therapist. For some couples, a certified sex therapist who is trained to sort out the psychological and physiological aspects of the problem may be advisable.

♥

HAVING FUN TOGETHER

Isn't having fun together the reason most couples got interested in each other in the first place? Because they found themselves having a great time with each other? Of course, it's a chicken/egg phenomenon. Did the fun together cause the infatuation to occur or did the infatuation make everything they did together seem like great fun? If the fun preceded the infatuation, there's a better chance it will still be there, however dormant, after the infatuation has run its course. In either case, if the relationship goes on long enough, the vicissitudes of everyday life will conspire to make having fun together a significant challenge at the least.

Todd called to cancel his appointment because he had to stay home with the baby while his wife, Leah, was in bed, recuperating from the flu. As a facetious aside, he commented, "Well, at least this will give Leah and me a few extra hours together of *quality* time."

It's typical for people with young children to go for long stretches without being alone for any significant time. And when it isn't the kids getting in the way of having "adult" fun time, there's the house cleaning and yard work, the time demands of your work, visits with relatives, colds and flu, you name it.

When the relationship is starting out you always manage to find time to be together, no matter how demanding your schedules and other responsibilities. Lots of time for long walks, exciting weekend trips, after-work cocktails, dinner, dancing, playing golf or tennis together, maybe even some mid-day escapades in a luxury hotel room. When's the last time you heard of a couple in a long-term relationship cavorting on a Wednesday afternoon at the Ritz?

But sooner or later, even the most playful couples can count on their work interfering with their having fun together. Modern work loads have been increasing for a decade. Time for fun gets harder and harder to eke out as the months roll by and it becomes clear that your less infatuated colleagues are working significantly more hours on the job, or that you're getting exhausted from burning the candle at both ends. Got to put in overtime, catch up on those business golf dates and business dinners, stay late at the office to get ahead on work or merely to catch up. Then it's home to the family, the kids leaping at you the minute you walk in the door. Pretty soon there's no time left.

Those of you without children aren't exempt either. As the relationship goes on longer and longer, if you're married or not married, with or without kids, it gets harder to find the motivation to have fun together. Debby reflects with bemusement on what happened to her and her boyfriend, Rob. "We used to play tennis all the time when we were first dating. We had great fun even though I wasn't nearly as good as Rob. It didn't matter. We'd laugh and joke; he'd give me some pointers; and we'd make sexy bets—like the winner could choose any sexual fantasy and the loser would have to act it out. But after a few months, Rob hardly ever wanted to play tennis with me. He'd tell me he just wasn't getting enough of a workout, or that there wasn't enough competition, or he had to play with some guys from work as a business obligation, or it's been a long time since he's gone out with the guys. And it wasn't only our tennis time that fell by the wayside."

You make a deal with the devil when you exchange having fun together for having most of your fun apart. When the fun together goes out of the relationship, your future happiness may be going out as well.

We do change over time, as do the circumstances of our lives. So what constitutes having fun together, or some good sex, in your relationships is bound to change over time too. But that doesn't mean that the general principle changes very much. At any stage, under almost any circumstances, a relationship is putting its best foot forward when a couple is having a decent amount of fun together and at least some satisfying good sex.

Times of tragedy will surely weaken the sex and fun pillars. It's unrealistic to expect joyfulness and misery to coexist, so it should come as no surprise that however close couples may be during crises, these same crises put the relationship at significant risk. We've all heard of the couples who broke up after the death of a child or a prolonged illness, or serious financial problems. In bad times couples need to lean heavily on the other two pillars: *conversation for understanding* and *fighting for the relationship*.

♥

CONVERSATION FOR UNDERSTANDING

The point of this kind of conversation is getting to know about, and keeping in touch with, each other's concerns, desires, needs, views, values, and ideas so as to add to a feeling of a shared bond. In the stage of infatuation, you imagine you can tell the person you "love" absolutely anything about yourself and you're completely open to accepting anything your lover should share. This belief is rarely tested, neither lover revealing too much, preferring the fantasy that you could if you wanted to. Instead, you incorporate the little you know (almost always very positive stuff) into some idealized inner vision. It isn't too often that your lover can actually live up to the ideal, so when the infatuation wanes and you begin to see the "real" person, you frequently end up feeling cheated, eventually moving on to a new "ideal."

To stop perpetuating that pattern, it's essential to establish this pillar of *conversation for understanding* right from the start. You have to really open up to the person you pretend you can say anything to. You have to encourage your lover to open up to you. Without any reality base, when your fantasy ends so does the relationship.

Understanding and feeling understood is of enormous help in keeping a relationship secure even in the tough times—when the romance dips, when problems develop, when crises occur. If you have shared openly you have forged a bond that provides a sense of security and develops a feeling of trust that you are there for each other.

Conversation for understanding is the kind of talk that says who you are and what you're about, not what your time schedule is. Conversation wasters and avoiders are legion.

For all those wily conversationalists so adept at manipulation in conversation, there are an equal or perhaps greater number of nonconversationalists. In my practice and in my personal life, I meet all too many couples who rarely talk about anything substantive because one or both members find it difficult to relate verbally, or one or the other "just doesn't know what to talk about" beyond the most mundane matters.

Does this mean you must bare your soul to your partner, tell your lover or marital partner everything? Should you let it *all* hang out? No. Much communication is neither constructive nor likely to create closeness. All too often communication is meant to hurt, insult, attack, demean. This will never lead to understanding, at least not the kind of understanding that brings a couple closer and allows feelings of trust to build.

When your partner begins a conversation with such lines as "Let me give it to you straight from the hip...," or "Not that I'm perfect or anything...," or "I'm only telling you this because you always said we should be honest with each other...," the only kind of understanding likely to be gained from what follows is that your partner has a need, conscious or unconscious, to alienate or hurt you, thus gaining some desired distance. Your partner is likely to be successful at the task, but fails miserably at the goal of communicating for the purpose of understanding.

The communicator's real intent is the crucial concept here. When the intent of a conversation is to wound, manipulate, discredit, and sometimes annihilate, this is communication at its most corrupting and destructive. This is exactly what I don't mean when I write about *conversation for understanding,* which is conversation that opens you up to your partner, inspires acceptance, tolerance, consideration, sympathy. This kind of conversation is key to achieving real intimacy. The more of this type of conversation you both participate in, the greater the degree of intimacy you attain.

Take my earlier example of Charlotte. When she admitted she was embarrassed and nervous about expressing her sexual needs to Mark and he responded by saying he wanted her to tell him because he wasn't a mind reader, this was the beginning of their communicating for the purpose of understanding. Instead of using communication to battle with each other, they were using it to inform and enlighten each other.

Most busy couples today, engaged in the balancing act of work, family life, and personal interests, end up spending much of their conversation time going over life management schedules. Who's got time for the car repair run, who is coming over and when, how to coordinate work, recreational meetings, civic responsibilities, and when there are children involved, who gets the kids where, spends time with the kids when, etc.? All the activities and responsibilities that interfere with sex and fun also interfere with time for meaningful conversation.

For many couples, conversation of the type I'm proposing is a lost art, for some an art they never even knew existed.

Earlier, I discussed Barbara and Steven, a couple married for eleven years, who hardly ever talked to each other. When Steven did the Smartcard sort he was amazed to discover how many issues there were that he'd enjoy talking about with his wife. Before, whenever Barbara badgered him about not talking more with her, he really had no idea what there was to talk about. His mind drew a blank. Not only wasn't he used to conversing for the purpose of understanding, he hadn't the foggiest idea what kind of conversing that would be. Until he did the Smartcard sort, he really had no concept of the large number of issues that went into the making up of a relationship that could be usefully discussed. Working with the Smartcards provided a training ground for him in the art of conversation for understanding.

Conversation for understanding needs to be an ongoing update on the topics you selected as positives, negatives, and unknowns. If all of those topics were to be included in every update, it's easy to see how the process could overwhelm even the couples who really make an effort at it. I advise you to select one or two Smartcards a week and set aside time to discuss those specific issues. Balance out positives and negatives, and don't let those issues you feel you'd like to know more about get lost in the shuffle. And always remember that your goal is to give and receive deeper understanding, not to win points at your partner's expense.

♥

FIGHTING FOR THE RELATIONSHIP

I tell couples that each partner has a sacred responsibility to guard the walls of their relationship from all perceived threats and bring up serious concerns so they can be resolved before they eat the relationship up alive. Anything that serious will be unpleasant and difficult to discuss. The timing will always be wrong. What's worse and far more damaging is to put it off.

Fighting for the relationship is vital to surviving and triumphing over the great threats to a happy pairing. This must be a conscious and intentional goal, because it's frightening work and requires commitment to the relationship over and above your individual egos.

The fighting part of fighting for the relationship doesn't mean having a knock-down-drag-out screaming match. It means problem-solving that focuses on the needs of the relationship as an entity, which are separate from the primary needs of the individuals. To reiterate, the needs of the relationship are, at a minimum, the four pillars—some good sex, having fun together, conversation for understanding, and fighting for the relationship, this last relying heavily on your achieving the other three. Your relationship has many other needs and demands which are very prudent to think about and discuss. As I've pointed out, most couples, especially when they're under stress, have difficulty sorting out all the tangled issues that are important to explore. The Smartcard sort can open the door to this process.

When I write about fighting for the relationship, I mean fighting *for* your happiness together, as well as fighting *against* threats to the relationship. Erecting this pillar and maintaining its solidity requires conscious effort to scrutinize it for signs of decay and to pool your resources to take care of problems as they arise. This is not a win-lose or even a win-win resolution for either of the partners, but rather a win-win resolution for the relationship itself. It's not what's best for either you or your partner, but what's best for your relationship. One or both of you may have to make some changes, shift some gears, make some compromises for the good of the relationship. Take an automobile that you invest a lot of money in and want to last a long time. I may like to speed, but that means too much wear and tear on the engine. You may prefer a red car to a white one, but red fades quicker and won't hold up as well. If the car is important enough to us we'll both make adjustments, because the car itself is worth more than color or speed.

The major issues couples fight over these days are fighting for enough time together, fighting for fidelity, fighting for independence that doesn't destroy the whole relationship in the bargain. Whenever you notice these or any other issues you think threaten your relationship as a whole, you must take up the fight.

In fighting for the relationship you're really fighting for your happiness. That means whenever either you or your partner notice that you're not as happy as you used to be, you need to stop and figure out what's wrong, what's missing, and/or what you've let slide by the wayside. In my own marriage and in advising other couples, I always stress that being happy together is well worth fighting for. You shouldn't settle for anything less. Even in time of hardship and tragedy, you can insist on being happy with how you, as a couple, are handling the grief.

Your relationship needs you to go beyond fighting for survival to fighting to be happy together and proud of your union.

♥

THE RELATIONSHIP FOUR SQUARE

I've developed another architectural paradigm that helps clarify the unequal roles of the four pillars. Please pardon my mixed metaphors. I call it the Relationship Four Square. Four square is a playground game I learned as a kid in the Bronx. My children played it growing up in the suburbs of Boston.

To play the game you draw a big chalk square on the ground and divide it into four equal-sized boxes. Players stand just beyond each of the outside corners and attempt to keep a playground ball bouncing in the boxes without going outside the lines.

Imagine that each of the boxes is labeled with the name of one of the pillars. There's a box called some good sex, and a box called having fun together; the third's called conversation for understanding, and the last, fighting for the relationship.

To maintain an effective intimate relationship you must keep the ball bouncing in each of the boxes, as in the game, but rather than having the ball land hit-or-miss in any of the boxes, as in the game, you must guide the ball to the right box at the right time.

CONVERSATION FOR UNDERSTANDING MOST OF ALL	**FIGHTING FOR THE RELATIONSHIP** WHENEVER THERE'S A SERIOUS THREAT
GOOD SEX SOMETIMES	**HAVING FUN TOGETHER** WHENEVER POSSIBLE

THE RELATIONSHIP FOUR SQUARE

The ball has to bounce in the some good sex box just enough to glue the relationship together—often for some, rarely for others.

It must bounce in the having fun together box with close to the same frequency as it did when you were dating each other.

The biggest task of this four square game is to keep the frequency of bounces up very high in the conversation for understanding box so you are sure you are known and understood by your partner. That's how you can believe you are loved for your true self.

Bounce the ball in the fighting for the relationship box whenever you perceive a significant threat to the heart of your union. This may never come up, but if it does you can't afford to miss your target.

CHAPTER TEN
SHIELDS THAT PROTECT GOOD RELATIONSHIPS

I like to think of love relationships as delicate hothouse flowers. They both need diligent care, tender attention, and healthy nourishment. And just like the hothouse flower, which must be protected from the elements, so, too, must our love relationships be protected from the strains and pressures that go hand in hand with intimacy, and be protected as well from the vicissitudes of everyday life. Like the well-constructed, temperature-controlled greenhouse that shields our flowers, we must create protective shields for our relationships. Putting these shields in place and applying them when necessary will ameliorate the pressures that naturally derive from spending so much time together in a close psychological interdependency. These shields should most especially be in place when discussing and exploring your Smartcard sorts with your partners.

♥

THE SLOW TALK SHIELD

Mutual understanding, achieved through good conversation and the healthy resolution of arguments, is the wellspring of romantic love.

Unfortunately couples' conversations are too often fertile territory for misunderstanding, lack of understanding, and dishearteningly ineffective communication. Most of the problem results from lack of clarity in expressing views or feelings, or from plain not listening. The potential for the problem usually gets worse during arguments. Some of us are instinctively driven to win arguments while others of us are ready to give up at the drop of a hat. This couldn't be more unfortunate because these alternatives rule out experiencing something special—the opportunity to feel truly understood, which then engenders a stronger sense of closeness, sharing, and commitment.

For over two decades now I've taught patients to overcome the fight/flight cycle with a technique I call **slow talk.** It's a straightforward process but a counter-intuitive one, so it takes a good deal of conscious effort to master it. The slow talk method is simple enough: When you get into a heated discussion or intense conversation with your partner, after making a point, have your partner summarize in his or her own words what you're saying. Is your partner's reading accurate? If not, rephrase it in a continuing effort to get your point or your feeling across. Again, have your partner paraphrase you. Keep it up until you feel sure you've been understood. In the same way, play back what you think your partner is saying so that your partner can confirm whether you've got the picture.

Before I give you an example of slow talk, here's a snippet of the more typical "fast talk" between partners.

> JACK: "Your mother's always putting me down. And you're just like her. You're never satisfied with anything I do."
> KELLY: "I'm sick and tired of you criticizing me and my mother. We're not the ones always finding fault. It's you."
> JACK: "Right. Twist it around. That's typical of you too. Always making me out the bad guy."
> KELLY: "If the shoe fits..."

In the above exchange, Jack and Kelly are off and running, throwing escalating jabs at each other, creating a series of unproductive and certainly uninformative attacks and counterattacks. What are they really fighting about? What's really troubling them? Slow talk gives them both the opportunity to find out.

Let's replay Jack's opening remark, this time responding with slow talk approach.

> JACK: "Your mother's always putting me down. And you're just like her. You're never satisfied with anything I do."
>
> KELLY: "You mean my mother always criticizes the way you do things around the house? And you think I'm very critical of everything you do?"
>
> JACK: "Not so much the things I do, really. It's more this attitude you both have that I'm not as good as your father was at looking after things around the house."
>
> KELLY: "You mean you think we're both always comparing you to my father?"
>
> JACK: "Your mother certainly does. And when you don't stick up for me, I think you're feeling the same way she feels. And that really hurts."
>
> KELLY: "So you're not really saying I'm critical of you. You're really saying that I'm not more supportive of you, especially in front of my mother. You'd like me to show my mother that I think you're doing just fine, thank you."
>
> JACK: "Yes. That's exactly what I'm trying to say. But now that we're talking about it, I realize it doesn't really matter to me what your mother thinks. I care about what you think. If I were more secure about that, I probably wouldn't get so worked up when your mother's around."

Slow talk takes a lot more time and effort, but in this conversation, Kelly and Jack are really getting at feelings and issues of concern that can ultimately give them a greater understanding of each other as well as bring them closer. Compare this method to fast talk, which served only to pull Jack and Kelly farther and farther apart.

Often in the course of slow talk you both gain the added advantage of thinking through your own feelings and thoughts on a deeper level. In the above example, Jack was able to see that it wasn't his mother-in-law's attitude that really troubled him, but his feeling that he needed more positive reinforcement from Kelly. That gives Kelly a chance to think about how she shows her support of Jack. By clarifying feelings or ideas for your partner, you're doing it for yourself as well.

If you faithfully follow this process you may not win the argument, or even solve each problem, but you'll have avoided a progression of misunderstandings and you'll come out of the discussion with increased trust in your partnership and the good feeling of knowing you've both been listened to and understood. That rare and precious experience is the essence of conversation for understanding. Instead of terminating a conversation or argument feeling frustrated, alienated, or misunderstood, you come away with the satisfaction of having really shared in a meaningful way, leaving you feeling closer to your partner.

When discussing your Smartcard sort with your partner, slow talk is crucial. This isn't easy because of the emotionally charged nature of finally having put all your cards on the table. Avoid the tendency to race ahead, which often forces your partner into a defensive position. Without slow talk, misunderstandings are rife and both of you can come out of the experience feeling more frustrated, embittered, and alienated than before. However, by employing slow talk as you discuss the feelings and issues surrounding each Smartcard, you and your partner have a unique opportunity to truly get to know each other in greater depth. You will feel understood as well as acquire the capacity to be more understanding, and enter into the spirit of a truly loving relationship, creating a special bond, and beating the odds.

♥

THE NO-HITTING-BELOW-THE-BELT SHIELD

Emily tells me Grady's a terrific guy, except when they're fighting. "Then he pulls out all the heavy artillery. As far as he's concerned, it's go for broke." Using the ARGUING AND FIGHTING Smartcard as her focal point, Emily selects all the negatives that are affected by the way Grady fights. These include BEING REASONABLE AND FAIR, BEING SUPPORTIVE, BEING COOPERATIVE AND SHARING, EXPRESSING LOVE, TRUSTING, BEING CONSIDERATE, CONTROL/LEADERSHIP ISSUES, PROBLEM-SOLVING STYLE, LISTENING, and EXPRESSING EMOTIONAL HONESTY.

Emily feels that Grady doesn't fight fair. He attacks her weaknesses, brings up things from the past that she's ashamed of, and if other people happen to be around, he'll think nothing of humiliating her in the course of a fight. As Emily says, "When he hits on something that really upsets me, he rubs it in. After a fight I feel as though I've been put through the wringer."

What Grady is doing is hitting below the belt. He and Emily have established no shield against this cruel and painful behavior. Virtually everyone has known since childhood that hitting below the belt is against the rules, but if my psychotherapy practice is any indication, too many people forget all about it when the relationship heat is on.

Without the no-hitting-below-the-belt shield in place, arguing and fighting becomes a very destructive force, the punches excruciating and devastating. Without this shield you end up fighting to win at all costs on the one side, and just trying to survive the verbal beating on the other. Under such harmful circumstances it becomes just too painful to fight for the relationship, thus putting the relationship itself in serious jeopardy. When hitting below the belt becomes a pervasive pattern in a relationship, with one or both partners cutting each other down in private and public, the chance for that relationship to flourish is just about nil.

♥

THE PHYSICAL PRIVACY SHIELD

You should have learned much of this behavior growing up—such simple courtesies as knocking when entering rooms with closed doors, having a place to go in the house when you need to be alone, respecting each other's belongings, not stepping on each other's toes. As an adult involved in a love relationship, you must be very conscious of your own need for physical privacy as well as that of your partner.

Often, when physical privacy is not respected in a relationship, it is reflected in many negative Smartcard choices. Sam moved in with Mary-Kate a year ago and one of his biggest complaints about the relationship is that he feels Mary-Kate has "moved in on all of my space." He says with exasperation, "She follows me around like a little puppy dog. Her clothes end up in my drawers. She uses my deodorant. I took to locking the bathroom door because she'd think nothing of walking in on me if she needed some makeup or whatever. When I tell her all this bothers me, she turns it back on me, telling me I have a problem with intimacy. She thinks there should be no locked doors between us, physically or emotionally."

When Sam does the Smartcards, focusing directly on this problem of physical privacy, he sees concretely how many issues in his relationship with Mary-Kate are negatively affected by this missing shield. These include BEING POLITE/CORDIAL, ANXIETY LEVEL ISSUES, BEING AFFECTIONATE, PERSONAL HYGIENE ISSUES, ISSUES IN HAVING

OR RAISING CHILDREN, ATTITUDE TOWARD PAST RELATIONSHIPS, EXPRESSING EMOTIONAL HONESTY, CARING ABOUT OTHER PEOPLE, BEING CONSIDERATE, BEING REASONABLE AND FAIR, and BEING COOPERATIVE AND SHARING—just to name a few. Only after Sam explores all of these issues does he realize how vital this shield is in order for him and Mary-Kate to live together.

The need for physical privacy is universal, but the size of the needed physical privacy shield will vary from couple to couple and can fluctuate depending on the stage of your relationship. When you're dating, you may or may not want your partner to spend the night at your place. You or your partner may be concerned about being "crowded." If you're living together or married, you may still want some space in the house you can call your own. You may not mind if your spouse shares your hairbrush, but you may well draw the line at sharing a toothbrush.

We don't all have the same requirements for privacy. Clearly, Sam and Mary-Kate have very different requirements, as well as different capacities, for sharing physical space and possessions. Mary-Kate wants to abandon this shield completely, all of the time, which only increases Sam's desire to both enlarge his shield and keep it firmly in place. After doing the Smartcard sort, Sam sees that he has to help Mary-Kate understand that her desire to remove all the "locked doors" is not encouraging intimacy. Quite the opposite. It's making him pull away from her. On the other hand, Sam needs to examine whether he's keeping too many doors "locked" as a way to keep from getting close.

Resolutely maintaining the privacy shield at all times can serve to keep intimacy at bay. While even in the most intimate relationships certain boundaries are established, they must be counterbalanced by a willingness to let your partner in some of the time, on some occasions.

As a writer, my wife, Elise, views her office as her private domain. When she steps inside that room and shuts the door, she is hanging an invisible "do not disturb" sign or privacy shield on the doorknob. I go to great pains to respect that shield, but since her office is at home it isn't always easy. If I do interrupt her, it's for what I consider good reason. She doesn't always agree. But she does recognize my concerted effort to honor her shield, so although we may argue over a given instance, we never argue over the issue in general. What's essential is that a reasonable need for physical privacy should be respected.

You must also guard against overusing the shield to keep intimacy at bay. Let's return again to Mary-Kate and Sam. While Sam at first correlates his excessive use of the shield purely as a response to

Mary-Kate's "intrusiveness," he does admit that he had mixed feelings in the first place about moving in with Mary-Kate. Was he really ready to take this step? Would he "open any more doors" with a woman who was less obtrusive? Is he willing to share any of his physical space? I point out that Mary-Kate may be overstepping the boundaries to compensate for him setting up so many of them. He acknowledges that I definitely have a point there. What Sam decides he must do is sort out how much of this is his issue before he talks the problem over with Mary-Kate.

Physical privacy extends beyond space and possessions to your and your partner's bodies.

Physical abuse and all forms of threatening words or behavior utterly breach the physical privacy shield. They constitute extreme examples of fatal flaws. Insisting on physical intimacy when your partner says no is a major threat to the relationship as a whole. Your partner needs to be confident that you respect her or his total right to say no to sex or any kind of physical intimacy at any given time. Forcing physical intimacy not only can be a criminal offense, but is always an unforgivable crime against any loving relationship. Unwanted seduction is the most insidious breach of the physical privacy shield. Many people make the mistake of thinking that everything is fine if the seduction is successful, but that is emphatically not the case when your partner has been coerced. The outcome of such seductions is a severe breach of trust which may create a **fatal flaw** in your relationship.

The physical privacy shield is especially handy when couples are fighting. Knowing you can come and go freely from your partner's space in time of tension means you don't have to go too far away for a breather. Once you regroup, you can reenter your partner's space and continue to fight it out.

♥

THE MENTAL PRIVACY SHIELD

Heather has been going with Craig for a couple of years. She says that the big problem that prevents them from getting really close is that Craig won't open up enough. She's utterly frustrated, after having done everything she can think of to "bring him out" to no avail. Craig is equally frustrated. He says that "Heather is constantly pounding on me, demanding I share every little thought or feeling with her. And if I don't she immediately interprets it to mean I'm holding back, keeping something from her. Don't I deserve any privacy?''

Absolutely. While Heather may have a legitimate complaint about Craig, her constant badgering and intrusiveness into his inner feelings only serves to make him more resentful, more closed, more removed.

The emotional privacy shield functions similarly to the shield that protects your physical privacy. Again, you run into serious problems regarding intimacy if you always have the emotional shield propped up. But you must be allowed to put it up at times. Having even the most open, sharing relationship doesn't mean you eliminate the emotional privacy shield altogether. You may choose to keep the shield in place for certain feelings, for a long time or even permanently. Some people experience the pressure to share too deeply about particularly sensitive or painful issues to be tantamount to rape.

Demands for emotional sharing at times when your partner is experiencing heightened stress may cause considerable anger or even more withdrawn behavior as a defense against the pain that the exploration of feelings might bring. Rather than press on and cause that pain, you need to honor the emotional privacy shield and find another more appropriate time or approach to explore those feelings. There's always a tomorrow in a good love relationship. It's one of the most powerful joys of commitment. It if hurts too much today, you can be sure of finding the opportunity in the future.

♥

KEEP YOUR SHIELDS SHINED

Armed with your four shields—slow talk, no hitting below the belt, respecting physical privacy, and respecting emotional privacy—you not only protect yourself and your partner against surprise attacks, but you protect the relationship itself.

CHAPTER ELEVEN

FEARS THAT THREATEN GOOD RELATIONSHIPS

A relationship is a delicate structure, pushed and pulled by our opposing inner drives. In discussing this concept with my patients, I like to paraphrase the title of Robert Heinlein's novel, *The Moon Is a Harsh Mistress*. My paraphrase is, A relationship is a harsh mistress. There are many analogies between Heinlein's story about the struggle to colonize the inhospitable moon and the toil and turmoil we go through in an effort to make our love relationships prosper and last. Heinlein explores how tough it would be to sustain and nurture life on a planetoid with no atmosphere, intolerable extremes of temperature, and little to no water—almost as tough as sustaining and nurturing a long-term, loving relationship in the inhospitable environment of everyday modern life compounded by our inner conflicts and confusions about romance, love, and intimacy. To make an environment for your relationship to survive in, you must create a way to give it time and attention, keep the extremes of your feelings under control, and protect it from harsh, even toxic, outer and inner forces.

The outside forces—the stresses and pressures of everyday life that assault the protective enclosure intimacy needs for its very survival—are relatively easy to identify: excessive time demands from any source and family, community, and national crises. The inner forces that can lethally poison the atmosphere most often take the form of deep-seated fears. These fears are elusive enemies, harder to recognize, understand, and come to terms with, thereby making them all the more powerful and treacherous obstacles to our striving for intimacy.

♥

The first three fears I'll discuss hinder the process of getting on with the day-to-day business of a love relationship. They keep you and your partner from grappling with how your relationship is going, impede facing necessary issues of concern, and prevent you from making needed changes. In today's psychological jargon, succumbing to these particular fears *disempowers* the relationship. These fears prevent you from taking steps to control in any significant way what happens to your relationship, so you are left adrift.

♥

WHEN YOU'RE AFRAID OF REJECTION

No sooner do many of you fall in love than you find yourselves consumed with the fear that your partners will fall out of love with you. You lock into a litany of anxiety-engendering self-doubts. Can anything that feels this good really last? I've never been lucky in love, so why should I suddenly get lucky now? If he or she really knew me would he or she still love me? This very litany sets you up to create negative feelings and actions that push your partners away.

What do you do to counteract this fear? You start walking on eggshells, bending over backward to please, looking and behaving the way you think your partner expects—all actions designed to counteract the possibility of your partner falling out of love with you.

Ironically, these efforts often prove to be your downfall. You can put your best foot forward only so long. What you don't realize is that your best foot is really your worst. And it's not stepping forward, it's stomping all over the relationship. Eventually the strain of pretense and subterfuge gets to you and you start to develop feelings of resentment, anger, and dependency-related states like depression and regression. Your partner ends up with hard feelings because of your negative attitude, not for anything to do with what you were afraid of in the first place.

The fear of falling out of love puts a lot of wear and tear on the fragile atmosphere of an intimate relationship. In the extreme, you can find yourself always on guard against saying or doing anything that you think will alienate your partner, and reacting with terror when your partner finds fault, or seems to be doing so.

Rhonda was so worried that Andrew would fall out of love with her that she took a rather casual remark about a former girlfriend of his being very thin as a direct attack on her. She was sure Andrew found her less pleasing than the woman he had previously been in love with. "I was convinced that he thought I was pudgy, so that when we had sex I felt very self-conscious. I was sure Andy was turned off by my weight." What was actually happening was that Rhonda was getting turned off. Andrew picked up on her discomfort and got to thinking that she didn't look forward to having sex with him. He was right, but for the wrong reasons. Having no idea about the real reason for Rhonda's disinterest, Andrew began pulling back from the relationship. Rhonda was causing the situation she feared. It was a self-fulfilling prophecy.

All too often, the tension that accompanies your fear of rejection leads you to set the rejection in motion. Some of you find the tension so distressing that you deliberately undermine your romantic relationships. You just know, in your insecurity, that you're going to get rejected, so you have to be one step ahead of your partner, doing the rejecting first. You ruin everything just to get the pain and heartache over with.

If you are given to relationship dependencies, in which your sense of self-worth, not to mention your very sense of existence, comes from feeling in love, or being loved, then the fear of falling out of love can come to haunt every aspect of your relationship. Indeed, it can infect every aspect of your life. This deep-rooted psychological conflict often results from being raised in a dysfunctional home where parental love could not be counted on—often in families in which there were severe drinking or drug problems, other types of mental illness, abuse and/or neglect.

A fair share of neglected children also spring from seemingly normal families with busy, successful working parents whose investment in their own careers leaves them little time for child-rearing. Many of us come from families in which both parents worked and had to juggle their careers and home life. We may not have gotten all the time and attention we wanted, but we got a fair share of it and can recognize that our parents made a concerted effort to attend to our needs. But I am referring here to parents who were so wrapped up in their own lives that they truly neglected their children's emotional needs even if they attended to their physical needs. These people may have functioned wonderfully outside the home, but as parents they came up significantly wanting.

When children are seriously neglected and grow up in the absence of a reassuring, reliable, loving environment, it creates the groundwork for dependency relationships in adulthood.

The fear of rejection escalates your inappropriate dependency behavior, which in turn gets you rejected. The hurt, depression, and loss of self-respect you experience from this rejection only serve to heighten your dependency needs and make you more desperate and more afraid of rejection the next time. The only way to break the cycle is to seek professional help or attend support groups that address the problem directly. You need to work your way back from a damaged past, go through the necessary healing process, and participate in a program of self-recovery so that you will not "self-destruct" your future relationships.

The fear of rejection may come sharply into focus when you consider whether or not to do the Smartcards with your partner, or even when you are doing the sort by yourself. Are there certain issues you're censoring? Are you unwilling to look too closely at the relationship because a part of you is already sure you're going to be rejected? Are you so afraid of rejection that you reject your partner before he or she rejects you? Is your Smartcard sort an honest interpretation of your relationship, or are you putting more Smartcards in the negative stack than actually belong there? Are you trying to prove to yourself that this isn't going to work?

Maybe what you're really saying is that you're afraid to give the relationship a chance, because you're so afraid of getting rejected. So you beat your partner to it. This does protect you from the possibility of getting rejected by your partner, but it also prevents you from the possibility of a terrific, long-lasting relationship. Facing the fear of rejection head-on will allow you to do the Smartcards more openly and honestly, and give you the chance to find out the true potential of your relationship.

♥

WHEN YOU'RE AFRAID TO FIGHT

Don't object, don't dispute, don't disagree, don't get too deep or you may end up in a fight that will destroy your relationship. These fears are near and dear to my heart, and my sister Jackie's, because we come from a family in which fighting between our parents virtually never took place. The crippling lesson we took away from their example was that there is something terribly wrong with couples fighting.

Elise's family background was very similar in that she, too, never once saw her parents get into a real fight. To this day it's no picnic for any of us to raise a concern we think will get our partner angry. But our strong belief in fighting for our relationships means we have to bring up problems or concerns. Actually, for Elise and me, the experience of the fight itself has never been particularly bad. Worse is the pre-fight fear, the feeling that "you never know what to expect," even though we have long since learned what to expect. But we push on anyway. Since our goal is to resolve the fight rather than for either of us to win it, we usually come out of a fight feeling a lot better and closer than when we began it.

Higher up on the fear scale are those of you that are positively terrified of fighting. Not just resistant or anxious, but flat-out, heart-stoppingly terrified. For some of you it's an actual phobia. Many of you with this phobia come from families in which the fighting was very abusive, even violent. Even when you've chosen mates more wisely than your parents did, you're still terrified of fighting because you connect it to the horrendous fights you witnessed as children. The more extreme and malicious your parents' fighting was, the more often you witnessed violence and viciousness, the greater the fear of fighting in your own adult relationship.

In your efforts to avoid fighting (even if your own partner is someone who would not embroil you in cruelty or violence) you settle for avoiding or denying conflict at all costs—even though the cost could be the relationship itself. Denial is where your mind deliberately doesn't tell itself something, so that you can't do anything about it. It's like the adage of burying your head in the sand to avoid danger, but denial is even more dangerous, because your mind won't even alert you to the danger in the first place. The Smartcards will alert you. But it will still take enormous strength and daring on your part to acknowledge it openly. It will take even more courage to discuss your Smartcard sort with your partner or do a sort together and share the results. Fighting is bound to occur. It might be wise to tackle only one issue at a time. And if the fear of fighting as a result is great, do it with a counselor present.

Should you come from a violent family and pair off with a hot-tempered mate, you have a very realistic cause to fear fighting. In your case learning to fight effectively and safely is the central task your relationship faces. Don't hesitate to seek help. Doing the Smartcards in a supportive environment can still lead to fighting and arguing, but you'll have the opportunity to learn how to fight without becoming overwhelmed or panicked. In the end, the benefits of doing the Smartcards in this setting are twofold. You get to overcome your fear of fighting, and you get to sort out problem areas in your relationship, thus building a closer, more supportive relationship with your partner.

♥

WHEN YOU'RE AFRAID OF CHANGE

Many of you cling to the status quo, standing by those familiar adages, "If it ain't broke, don't fix it" and "Why upset the apple cart?" It feels immeasurably less risky to stick with what you have, even if it's not so hot, then to risk changes that could make things worse. It's the old "leave well enough alone" stance, even if, in truth, things aren't going all that well. Indeed, "why rock the boat?" "Why go looking for trouble?" Amazing, isn't it, all the clichés that support the fear of change?

If you succumb to a fear of change in your relationship, the most that will happen is that you won't see the changes when they come. Face it, whether you fear change or not, ignore it or not, like it or not, change occurs. What won't be changing is how you cope with problems that arise, how you relate to your partner, how you expect your partner to relate to you.

By not facing the reality of change head-on and making adaptations, alterations of behavior, and new compromises, you end up putting an invisible wedge between yourself and your partner. The relationship itself starts to stagnate. The energy dissipates. And what happens? You struggle desperately to get things back to the way they were. You try to pull the relationship back instead of propelling it forward.

Ironically, the harder you cling to the status quo, the more the relationship changes, invariably for the worse. Your fear incapacitates you, preventing you from providing input or influencing the changes that are taking place. It also prevents you from working cooperatively with your partner to fashion a closer relationship which evolves from the two of you coping successfully with change.

And even as you're spouting the adage, "If it ain't broke, don't fix it,'' you may be blind to the reality that it already *is* ''broke.'' Putting your cards on the table invites consideration of the many changes by vividly highlighting the positives and negatives in the relationship. Have they already shifted? Are the negatives worse than you had admitted to yourself? Are there fewer positives than you'd imagined?

Overcoming the fear of change takes you a giant step closer to examining and evaluating your relationships honestly. The Smartcards are a conduit for examining the changes, deciding what they mean to you and what you want to do about them once you've faced their existence. They provide you with the opportunity to get out of dead-end relationships, or add new life and vigor to relationships of worth.

♥

Now let's turn our attention to the fears that involve learning things about yourself or your partner that you may not want to admit to or feel you can't cope with. These potent fears reduce conversation for understanding to a bare minimum. You don't want to risk learning too much because it might raise legitimate concerns or play into neurotic fears you're trying to cover up. If you are experiencing some reluctance to putting your Smartcards on the table, it may well be that you are motivated by one or more of the following fears.

♥

WHEN YOU'RE AFRAID TO FIND OUT YOU'RE NOT COMPATIBLE

It's sensible for lovers to fear incompatibility, just like the fear of falling from high places would be real enough for mountain climbers. But you can't get the exhilaration of the climb without risking a fall. And you can't expect to have an enduring love relationship without risking some revelation, even though it means discovering some significant differences, and tolerating certain areas of incompatibility.

The fear of incompatibility can be so great that you engage in very little conversation for understanding, terrified that what you'll come to understand is that you're really not suited to each other—that you've made a dumb, foolish, and/or dangerous choice. The sad outcome of giving into this fear is a cool, distant relationship, one in which you couldn't tell if you were badly matched or the most compatible duo on the face of this planet.

WHEN YOU'RE AFRAID OF DISCOVERING OR UNCOVERING INSURMOUNTABLE PROBLEMS

Much of your confidence in your ability to cope effectively with problems in a relationship comes from what you learned or didn't learn as a child. Some of you, as children, brought a personal problem home seeking help from an immature, inebriated, or emotionally disturbed parent and ended up in a worse pickle by far than before you mentioned it. Some of you have witnessed parents dissemble before your eyes over a problem area such as an affair, gambling, or drug/drinking abuse that is brought out into the open. On a lesser but still significant scale many of you were told by a parent or sibling not to mention things that would upset mom or dad. Many of you have grown up thinking that if you couldn't cope with problems when you were kids, and if your parents couldn't, why should you be able to cope with them as adults?

Renée has been married for thirty-two years. She describes her husband as a good man who works hard for his family and makes few demands. She concedes that he can be gruff and insensitive at times, but she simply ignores him when he gets that way. Her children are all out of the home now and, left alone with Lionel without having the children as buffers, Renée has become depressed and agitated. When Renée does a Smartcard sort, her fatal flaws stack belies her minimizing: ATTITUDE ABOUT MORALITY, USING/ABUSING DRUGS AND ALCOHOL, and MENTAL HEALTH ISSUES are on the table. It turns out that this good breadwinner who's sometimes gruff and insensitive has a serious drinking problem, has had several affairs about which he's boasted to his wife, and has periodic bouts of paranoia and is sometimes delusional.

Renée breaks down and sobs as she talks about these fatal flaws for the first time. She's now able to see not only Lionel's serious problems but her own codependency. What makes her the saddest is all the years she let go by without taking any action. She paid an awful price for her fear of acknowledging and taking on such a difficult problem.

Sometimes, even though you're aware of a terrible problem, it isn't advisable to bring it up with your partner. After Renée did her Smartcard sort and became aware of her husband's fatal flaws, she had good reason to believe that he had deteriorated to the point of easily becoming physically violent if she confronted him. Instead, Renée sought help and support in a codependency group as well as joining Alanon. With their advice and support she was eventually able to approach her husband and broach the issue of his drinking. After a period of months spent encouraging him to join AA and see a psychiatrist but getting nowhere, Renée decided to leave him and get a divorce.

If you are involved in a potentially abusive relationship like Renée's, tread lightly. Should your Smartcard sort come up with many negatives that represent terrible problems, dangerous situations, or utterly unbroachable topics, think carefully before proceeding to involve your mate in your observations.

> **If your partner is threatening or even potentially violent, *do not do the Smartcard sort together*, except under the auspices of a psychotherapist as part of a formalized treatment plan.**

♥

WHEN YOU'RE AFRAID OF ALIENATION

The kind of conversation that creates closeness also highlights differences. Sometimes the prospect of finding out that you and your partner are incompatible is not only frightening in its own right, as I discussed earlier, but it leads to more deep-seated panic and a fear of alienation.

The fear of discovering that you and your partner are incompatible is merely the fear of the death of the romantic illusion that love makes you one forever. If there are too many differences between you, then you fear that the romance is at risk.

The fear of alienation is a much deeper emotion than the fear of losing your romantic illusions. The fear of alienation is akin to the inordinate fear of death. It's related to the idea that you came into the world alone and you die alone, and in between you seek companionship, love, connectedness. But some touch of inner truth tells you that you remain always alone, separate from all other beings on the earth. Just as some of you find contemplating death to be an unbearable activity, others of you are terrified of contemplating your essential aloneness even when you're in an intimate relationship.

The very fear of alienation can be so powerful that you end up getting scared of the closeness itself. If you have been using the relationship to overcome neurotic feelings of alienation in the first place, you could end up in the ironic predicament of running away from intimacy in order to avoid alienation. Not a satisfactory solution.

A better approach to overcoming the fear of alienation is to pick the Smartcard issues you care most about and stick with your discussion of them, despite your feelings of alienation, until you and your partner both feel fully understood. Once again, it might be best to do this with a therapist present.

Feeling fully understood is a strong reinforcement for feeling connected with your partner. That feeling of being linked engenders feelings of trust, affection, cooperation, honesty, consideration, and love. All of these feelings can effectively fend off feelings of alienation.

CHAPTER TWELVE

AVOIDING
THE PITFALLS

Just as there are fears that keep you from getting close, there are also attitudes and behaviors that create distance between you and your partner, ultimately squashing your chances for achieving a loving relationship. Much of the time, you may not even be aware of some of these attitudes and behaviors. You get into a wrong mental gear, don't realize the strain it's causing, and no one's out there telling you you've got to shift gears or you're sunk. If you're in one of the following gears, get the message—SHIFT!

♥

DISRESPECTFULNESS

When I was a child, growing up during the Golden Age of television, TV wives treating their TV hubbies without respect was a kind of standard joke. We got plenty of chuckles from shows like ''I Love Lucy'' and ''Life of Riley'' where the message got drummed in again and again that husbands and dads were just big, good-hearted lugs who needed to be tricked, cajoled, bamboozled, and ignored—for their own good and everyone's best interests. When my kids were growing up, TV was still giving the same lesson in shows like "The Jetsons" and "The Flintstones."

Not that it's all been one-sided by any means. Men got their licks in my parents' day in shows like "The Burns and Allen Show" in which poor Gracie was so sweetly stupid that George had to condescend to keep a special eye on her and her dim-witted schemes. And the tradition continued with "All In the Family," which managed to take disrespect of women (and everyone else) to new heights. It was an honest attempt to show how obnoxious that behavior was, but somehow the perpetrators' behavior ended up amiably tolerated and accepted.

Disrespect may get chuckles on TV, but in the real world disrespect is a killer of love. We can be disrespectful in any number of ways, both verbally and nonverbally. We show our partner disrespect when we don't call to say we'll be coming home late. We show it when we make a disparaging remark about our partner in public. We display a lack of respect when we belittle, insult, disregard, or deliberately embarrass or demean the one we love.

Annette, a hairdresser who recently returned to work, confronts this problem directly when she ranks ATTITUDE TOWARD WORK AND EARNING A LIVING first in her negative stack. Lyle has made it clear to her and to their friends that he finds her profession "frivolous." "He takes away all my pride in what I do by belittling it, making me look like a jerk or something because I enjoy being a stylist. When I tell him what I do makes people feel better about themselves, he laughs right in my face. And if he wants to do something on a Saturday, he just thinks I should call in and say I'm not coming into work, because, after all, I'm not, as he puts it 'saving the planet or anything.' "

Lyle's disrespect in this and other areas has resulted in Annette distancing herself from him as a protection against embarrassment, humiliation, and rage. But those feelings are there, bottled up inside of her. Now that she's put her cards on the table, she realizes that she has to deal with Lyle about the disrespectful way he's treating her.

♥

RUDENESS

We spend so much of our time having to "watch our step" and our manners—with our bosses and colleagues, with our employees, with our parents and in-laws—that we often feel we have a right to "let it all hang out" in our own homes with our own partners.

Winnie, a real estate agent, brushes off her rudeness to her husband with such comments to me as, "When I get home from a tough day of taking it from all sides I'm in no mood to put up with a pack of crap from my husband. I'm damned if I'm not going to say exactly what I think and feel to him. What's the point of being married if he doesn't love me enough to accept me the way I am?" Instead, Winnie should be saying, "I love this person, so I treat him better than I treat anybody else." That not only makes more sense, but makes for happier, healthier relationships.

Rudeness is a blatant irritant. It's a block to closeness simply because it's natural not to want to get close to a source of pain. Rudeness destroys the positive atmosphere necessary to do problem-solving in any situation. If you've fallen into the habit of treating your partner rudely, or you're being treated rudely yourself, take up your Smartcards and sort out the issues that are affected by the rude behavior. I guarantee you'll have a lot of food for thought, and more important, for discussion.

♥

AVOIDING FEELINGS

The communication of feelings is essential for mutual understanding. Feelings are our primitive, gut-level reactions to practically everything we think, do, or perceive. If your partner only knows your ideas and doesn't know what your unique feelings are about significant issues, then an important part of you stays hidden away from the relationship. Your partner will never know the whole story about you. And you'll never feel truly known and loved for who you really are. Problems that seem to have been rationally resolved may continue to crop up when contrary feelings that have been ignored continue to influence your behavior.

Often, the problem is that you don't know what you're feeling or even that you are feeling a certain way. You may compensate through the use of **projection**, a nonconscious psychological process by which you take feelings that you don't admit to and credit them to your partner. You may blame your partner for being testy when, really, you're the one in a foul mood. And since the entire process is *not* conscious, it's never immediately clear which partner might be doing the projecting. Often you end up blaming each other, never really getting down to the actual feeling, and even more important, never getting around to discussing it as a way of adding to your understanding of each other and of yourself.

My male patients struggle more with acknowledging or sharing feelings than do my female patients, with the exception of anger, which many men view as a "legitimate" feeling. Expressing other feelings, such as exuberance, joy, hurt, fear, and anxiety, is considered to be a show of weakness. "Big boys don't cry," we guys have been told again and again. When we slip up as kids, we've got our peers there to rub it in: "Cry baby, cry baby." We quickly learn to say, "Sticks and stones may break my bones, but words will never harm me." And by the way, when those stones are thrown, we'll be damned if we're gonna cry! After all, our mothers are telling us, "Do you see your father crying?" Rarely, if ever, have we seen our fathers cry, we must admit. Dad learned from his folks exactly what we learned from ours. We incorporate these messages as direct instructions to suppress hurt feelings or suffer humiliation.

Boys are not entirely alone in receiving these pernicious lessons. Plenty of girls get a similar message, which is to learn to be thick-skinned and suppress their feelings. So lots of the boys and some of the girls grow into adults who don't acknowledge unpleasant, painful, or embarrassing feelings.

Sometimes we suppress our feelings out of the fears I discussed earlier, but sometimes we've simply learned the lesson so well that we can't get in touch with our feelings even when we want to. The roadblocks remain stubbornly in place despite our wish to transcend them.

When your discussions center around your feelings, you don't have to defend yourself the way you might if it were about a decision or a point of view. If you're sad, you're sad. It may call for an effort at understanding on the part of your partner, but the truth of your emotion stands on its own power.

Use the Smartcard sort as a shortcut to teasing out your feelings and helping you get in touch with them. Look at each Smartcard in turn, thinking about events in your life that have a bearing on the card. If an issue provokes a memory to which you can attach a feeling, put the card on the table to create an **emotions stack.** These emotions can be positive or negative, happy, sad, upsetting, etc.

Grant, a man who has difficulty acknowledging and expressing his feelings, takes the ISSUES IN HAVING OR RAISING CHILDREN card in hand and talks about the birth of his daughter, how scared he was at first because his wife was in so much pain, and how moved and excited he felt when the doctor held the healthy baby up for him to see for the first time. Next on Grant's emotions stack is BEING REASONABLE AND FAIR. He recounts recently losing out on a promotion at work even though he was next in line for the new job. He still feels angry and resentful. Later, he goes back to this card and lifts it up. "It's not hard for me to admit being angry at being passed over for that promotion. What's hard to admit is that I feel humiliated and ashamed, especially around colleagues and my family. Like I wasn't good enough; like I can't make the grade; like I let them down." Tears well up in Grant's eyes. He's surprised, commenting that he hasn't cried since he was a kid. By the time Grant is finished with the task, he has ten cards on his emotions stack. He then ranks the cards by the strength of the feelings the issues evoke, allowing him to see that he not only has more emotions than he had previously recognized, but that they run the full gamut.

♥

EXAGGERATING YOUR FEELINGS

Some of you exaggerate your feelings, or feel your emotions with such intensity that it interferes with serious conversation. Every problem becomes a major confrontation involving massive emotions. Like the boy who cried wolf, you make it impossible to tell your serious concerns from your minor ones. You might be demonstrating a sign of this tendency if your Smartcard sort yields a large number of negatives that you have trouble ranking below the top of the stack. Of course, it's possible you have the worst relationship imaginable and that's where all the severe negatives come from. When you select a monster stack of serious negatives, subject your emotionality to some searching self-evaluation. Have many relationships ended explosively for you? Have friends and lovers complained you were too critical, too often disappointed, too angry about too many things? Are you constantly upset over your relationships, even friendships?

As you might guess, a partner who is extremely emotional and one who is out of touch with feelings make for the worst combination. Perry and Rachel are a perfect example. Perry tells me that before he met

Rachel, he "felt kind of dead inside, empty. My life was all work and all pressure. Rachel was so full of life, just being with her energized me. She really shook things up for me, kept things spinning. It was like being high." And what was it about Perry that drew Rachel to him? "I was feeling pretty fly-away, running on pure nervous energy when I met Perry. He seemed so solid, so together, a real rock of a guy. I thought he would help ground me, calm me down."

After they'd been together a while though, Perry says, "She was always on, always wanting to mix it up. She started in on me first thing in the morning and she'd still be at it when I was trying to get to sleep. Everything about me seemed to bug her. I couldn't even breathe right for that woman." Rachel counters, "Perry had to be the most sullen, withdrawn man I've ever met. I really think the guy's devoid of feelings."

Both Perry and Rachel concede that they "bring out the worst in each other." The more expressive and explosive she is, the more sullen and withdrawn he gets. The more he retreats into himself, the more abandoned and alone she feels and the more emotionally demanding she becomes.

When they each do a Smartcard sort for how they first viewed their relationship and compare that with how they view their relationship now, they can quite literally see the radical shift from positive to negative on many issues, especially HAVING FUN, HAVING CONVER-SATIONS, ARGUING AND FIGHTING, PROBLEM-SOLVING STYLE, BEING REASONABLE AND FAIR, LISTENING, BEING ROMANTIC, and MOOD AND EMOTIONAL ISSUES.

If you are involved in this type of emotionally divergent relationship with hardly any redeeming positives, the cold, hard truth is that the cards are stacked against you. The odds aren't in your favor for being able to erect and maintain any of the pillars for a solid, enduring relationship. Your best bet is to see the "writing on the cards" before you get too deeply enmeshed in a doomed relationship. It may be hard to get out while you're still clinging in some degree to your infatuation, but it's worth considering jumping ship as early on as possible. You'll be preventing a lot of pain and very likely lawyers' bills not so far down the road.

Occasionally, when I've done the Smartcard sort with people who have intense negative feelings about their partner, and yet these nega-tives are balanced by strong positives, one of the difficulties becomes prioritizing their feelings. Every negative not only gets exaggerated, but is viewed with equal intensity. They're all seen as "bad," period. Often, this intensity has less to do with actually believing each negative is equally problematic, equally stressful, equally important, than with the tendency to see negatives and/or positives in very black-and-white terms. Before you can explore the issues that concern you, it is important to see the gradations of gray. Some negatives are worse than others. Some positives mean more than others. It is essential to get a realistic picture of your relationship in order to evaluate it and tackle concerns realistically.

If you suffer from feeling equally strongly about almost every issue, you can use the Smartcards to practice spreading out the range of your emotions. When you're getting ready to initiate an argument, sort through the Smartcards, take out the ones from the areas you want to fight about, and force yourself to order them by how upset you are about each of the problems. If you're concerned only about one issue, pull out the other cards that are affected in some way by that issue and force yourself to rank them.

Much the same process will help individuals who can't differentiate their emotions because the intensity is always so low. Sort and rank the cards for intensity of emotion, forcing yourself not to give any two cards the same ranking. Should a large number of cards fall into a discard stack, take those cards and force yourself to choose to place them in either your emotionally positive or emotionally negative stack and then force yourself to rank each of the stacks for the strength of your emotion about each card.

♥

OVER-COMPETITIVENESS

"When we were first together we thought being competitive with each other was a plus," Trish, a young lawyer, tells me about her relationship with Mel, a business consultant. "We've always been very aggressive, go-for-broke people and we thought our drive to succeed—well, really to beat each other out—made us both stay on our toes. We applied the pressure in every area—who could get promoted faster, who could earn the most money, who could win on the tennis court, even who got more attention at a party." Trish goes on to explain that this pressure was rarely, if ever, openly verbalized. If it had been, it might have helped them both see the destructive impact it was having on their relationship. Always trying to keep the edge often left Trish or Mel stepping on the other's toes. And because both were so intent on the "win," they got into serious conflicts when Mel wanted to make a location move that would jump his career up another notch. Trish refused because it would have meant missing out on a promotion at her law firm. Mel gave in, but he was resentful—and all the more driven to "come out on top anyway."

When they do the Smartcard sort in my office, they lock horns at almost every drop of a card. They immediately step into competitive overdrive, trying to score points. Even small issues become "negotiating points." Over-competitiveness has trapped Trish and Mel into an inevitable lose-lose situation. They have plenty of desire to fight, but they haven't the faintest idea or appreciation of the art and the craft of fighting for the relationship. They've become super competitors, but a lousy couple.

It's a lonely competitive world out there and one of the wonderful things about a good love relationship is how it makes you members of a winning team, pulling together for the good of each other and the relationship. Sadly, when the competitive attitude comes into the relationship it leaves a lot of hurt in its wake. You just don't expect to have the ball stolen from you by a member of your own team.

The opportunities for over-competitiveness are everywhere; competing over the time and affection of friends and family, competing for the love of children, competing to be the one that's right, competing to be the most successful—and resenting the success of the other. There are many couples like Trish and Mel with whom competition takes place over everything: attention, money, space, you name it.

I have Trish and Mel do a second Smartcard sort, this time with the specific purpose of exploring their over-competitiveness. I ask them to sort out the issues that are positively and negatively affected by the competitiveness in their relationship. There are actually a few areas in which their competitiveness is a plus, such as ATTITUDE TOWARD TIME—they agree the competition keeps them both prompt for appointments and dates—and HANDLING MONEY—they compete successfully to be good money managers. Trish adds to her positive features stack HOBBIES AND OUTSIDE INTERESTS; she stuck with racquetball until she could sometimes beat Mel and ended up loving the sport. Mel, interestingly enough, puts MAKING A COMMITMENT TO THE

RELATIONSHIP in his positives—he's damned if he'd give Trish the satisfaction of thinking he quit on their marriage.

Their negatives, however, greatly outweigh their positives. These include EXPRESSING FEELINGS/HAVING FEELINGS, HAVING FUN, HAVING CONVERSATIONS, SEXISM ISSUES, EXPRESSING EMO-TIONAL HONESTY, EXPRESSING NEEDS, LISTENING, SETTING GOALS, BEING SUPPORTIVE, BEING ROMANTIC, ISSUES IN HAV-ING AND RAISING CHILDREN, BEING AFFECTIONATE, ARGUING AND FIGHTING, CONTROL/LEADERSHIP ISSUES, and BEING CO-OPERATIVE AND SHARING.

A number of the Smartcards in their negatives overlap, while others prove more an issue for one or the other of them. But what is of prime importance is that both Trish and Mel can see a comprehensive, honest picture of how vast and devastating their drive to compete has become and how deeply it has pervaded and perverted their quest for love and happiness together.

♥

P.S.: AVOID THE STRONG, SILENT TYPES

A word of advice for women who are attracted to the strong, silent type: *careful!* Your instincts and your best interests are fiercely at odds. Too often, I've seen patients in my office who are repeatedly attracted to this type. They think these men are more alluring, more self-assured, more powerful. As I tell my patients, their predilection is usually due to a combination of conditioning and fantasy. In the infatuation stage, the strong, silent men appear less threatening and less demanding, leading women to endow them with any qualities they desire.

The strong, silent type has been a cult romantic hero running through our folklore, our history, our popular fiction, and our movies. We've got the lone cowboy taming the West with his faithful horse and trusty rifle, we've got Cathy swooning over the practically mute Heathcliff on the pages of *Wuthering Heights,* and the likes of John Wayne and Clint Eastwood making their female costars and a host of women viewers take them eagerly to their hearts. We have idolized them and idealized them for ages, imbuing them with a whole parade of wonderful qualities.

The problem is, once the wild attraction wanes, it often turns out that the man can't communicate on any level beyond sex. When you do the Smartcard sort for a relationship with this kind of man you'll be shocked at how many cards end up in the unknown stack, no matter how long the two of you have been involved. As Susan who broke up with one of those strong, silent types commented, "I thought he was self-aware, but, if he was, he sure kept it to himself. I ended up feeling cheated."

In my practice I see many lonely, isolated women who are struggling in relationships with this type of man. And I also treat many depressed silent men. During couples work with these individuals, the Smartcard sorts have proven to be a most helpful technique. Without endless palaver, in fact, with almost no talking at all, these men can use the Smartcards to lay out their feelings and ideas about the state of their relationships. On several occasions, in response to a wife's plea, "Can't you tell me anything about what's bothering you about us?," her husband has held a particular Smartcard aloft and pointed to it speechlessly with his other hand. Sometimes a Smartcard can speak a thousand words—or at least start you off on the process.

CHAPTER THIRTEEN

THE FIVE GOLDEN RULES FOR LOVING SMART

In my twenty-five years in counseling, I've been continually appalled at how small a role ethics seems to play in the conduct of intimate love relationships. I blame those myths we cling to that falsely imply that ethical behavior comes automatically with love. I blame our upbringing and the role models provided for us. I blame the psychological, physical, and economic pressures of everyday life. Powerful, multiple forces do work upon us, often from opposing directions, making it hard to figure out what's right to do at any particular time.

Everyday life presents endless obstacles to maintaining high standards of ethics. In many instances, it's incredibly difficult to discern the most worthy course. Further, there's often a big price to pay for your ethical stance, as you'll have to compete at an unfair disadvantage in an unethical world of cut-throat competition.

Your love relationships can, should, and must be a refuge from the crudities and vagaries of the outside world, and they provide you with your very best opportunity to be the kind of person you most respect and admire.

Love without ethics is doomed to bring disappointment, pain, even despair. Sadly, love without ethics is no rarity. Even in the throes of infatuation, couples frequently treat each other shabbily, disrespectfully, callously. I have seen couples *in love* who treat the mailman better than they treat each other.

It's a sad state of affairs, if you'll pardon my double entendre. And what's especially sad is that the solution can really be quite simple. As simple and as basic as following the good old Golden Rule: Do unto others as you would have others do unto you. Maybe it sounds trite, but it's morally perfect and psychologically sound. You need to treat your partner as well as you wish to be treated and insist on the same treatment in return.

My Five Golden Rules for Loving Smart are a set of basic guidelines for the primary worthy, humane behaviors that benefit love relationships the most. You might want to think of them as a kind of secular list of commandments for lovers. I'm certainly not going to claim that God will punish you for not following them, but I'm fully prepared to predict that your love life will be more rewarding and joyful if you heed these rules.

♥

1. THE RULE OF REASONABLENESS

Reasonableness in a love relationship means not taking extreme stands at the expense of your partner's interests and, sometimes, even your own. We all have arguments, disagreements, differences of opinion. Being reasonable means accepting what makes the most sense over wanting to win, prove a point, or get the advantage. Being reasonable means that fights never end in outrageous threats, conflicts are worked out in a thoughtful manner, neurotic hang-ups are never sufficient in and of themselves to rule out a reasonable wish of yours or your partner's.

A well-established attitude of mutual reasonableness allows you to wade into potentially explosive problems knowing that neither of you is going to come out seriously burned. Assiduously adhering to the rule of reasonableness won't rule out disappointment, hurt, or bad arguments, but it will inject an extra element of vigor, faith, and resiliency that lets you surmount tough crises together without having to watch your back.

2. THE RULE OF CORDIALITY

Closeness has a way of stepping on your mental and physical feet. A cordial manner smoothes over the rough edges and establishes pleasant, respectful patterns of behavior that make the closeness bearable for longer stretches of time.

There's an open field for irritation and annoyance within close relationships. The entire process of developing and maintaining a love relationship is fraught with occasions of friction, tension, and hurt. If you're dating, you have to cope with getting to know each other, with the vulnerability that comes with revealing hidden parts of yourselves. You don't know what to expect for a reaction, and there's always that lurking fear of rejection.

If you're living together you suffer the frictions of proximity. You share the same bed—negotiating for space, covers, maybe dealing with snoring or differing sleep patterns. You share the bathroom, where you easily get in each other's way or move items that then can't be readily found. When you're living together even eating is a matter for negotiation, whereas living alone you eat what and when you please.

In a relationship you have to put up with your partner's less than perfect relatives, friends, moods, attitudes, needs. And your partner in turn has to cope with yours.

Living in this thorny jungle the salving balm of cordiality—everyday good manners—keeps us from stomping on each other's toes and imbues our interactions with dignity.

♥

3. THE RULE OF KINDNESS

Who should you be kind to if not the one you've chosen over all others? It certainly makes the world of sense to me that I treat the ones I love the most with the greatest benevolence. But, for many couples, it doesn't work that way at all.

Take Bess, who is in tears as she confronts her husband, Al. "You'll do anything for your damn mother. And when it comes to your friends or the guys down at the plant you can't do enough for them. You bend over backwards for every Tom, Dick, and Harry. Everybody's always telling me what a great guy you are. But if I ask you for the simplest favor, you can't be bothered, it's too late, or it's too early, or you're tired, or you accuse me of being too demanding or too controlling. You treat me like I'm nothing special to you.''

How is the delicate flower of infatuation to be rekindled again and again in such an inhospitable, unkind environment? It isn't. Thanks to Al's disregard, Bess, like many others in her situation, may find herself all too ready to succumb to the kindnesses of another guy!

The value of kindness is a hard notion to come by if you were almost never treated kindly as a child, or rarely saw your parents treat each other kindly. Even if your intention is to be kind to your loved one, you need the reinforcement of kindness in return. Anyone can get resentful and feel foolish about being the only nice one—the only one disposed to being helpful and sympathetic. Pretty soon no one's kind at all. Once things reach that point, the relationship is rushing pell-mell downhill.

♥

4. THE RULE OF FAIR PLAY

You're truly blessed if you have a partner who believes in fair play when it comes to love. It means that your partner will never exaggerate needs or manipulate dishonorably to get his or her own way. It means the resources you've created together will be shared equitably. It means you'll face conflicts and problems with your mutual interest at heart instead of self-interest and prejudice.

A history of fair play maximizes the chances of teamwork within a love relationship. A pattern of fairness creates an environment of trust, and in the long-term relationship that trust steadily builds deep respect that makes you *want* to love your partner.

♥

5. THE RULE OF COMPROMISE

If you know each other well and express your needs and wishes freely, chances are you'll often want to do different things at the same time or do the same things differently. Resolving these differences often requires some vigorous discussion and/or arguing, which is fine. What's not okay, though, is to fight repeatedly to the death to determine a winner. Or to throw your hands up in defeat and go off to your separate corners—and commence leading separate lives.

In our competitively oriented society compromise is easily and frequently confused with losing. Some men think that compromising with their girlfriend or wife is another way of saying they've given in. Giving an inch or two or even three isn't giving in. Not if both partners are moving closer toward a middle ground. Nor is compromise a sign of weakness one step removed from inviting slavery.

Compromise is one of the high arts of relating. The trick is to conceptualize the compromise as resolving a difference *in favor of the relationship*. This should remind you of the concept I introduced earlier of fighting *for* the relationship. Working together to devise a meaningful compromise teaches the skills you will need should you ever have to actually fight for the relationship. Since no couple will ever see eye-to-eye on everything, you'll have endless opportunities to practice the art of compromise. The more practice the better.

A successful compromise has another excellent side effect—it's a drug-free, relationship-bonding high. It's the kind of high that can actually lead to your feeling full of optimism, hopeful for your future together—downright infatuated, in the best sense. It's the nicest kind of irony that compromise, which can have such a bad rap, is really the most powerful of all the relationship reinforcers.

In the course of doing the Smartcards, one negative issue that received high priority for Fran and Brett was ATTITUDE TOWARD VACATIONS. As it turned out, this was a burning issue because the couple had finally saved enough money for a down payment on a vacation home. The conflict arose because Fran wanted a place in the mountains where she could ski and Brett, an avid sailor and wind surfer, wanted to be by the ocean. Both of them realized that they were on the verge of turning what was to be a wonderful gift for their hard work and sacrifice into a marital quagmire. A creative compromise was their only hope. In the end, they opted for a house on a large lake twenty minutes from good skiing and less than two hours away from the ocean. Fran and Brett not only averted disaster, they came up with a compromise that was even better than what either of them had first been so invested in having. They were rightfully proud of their problem-solving skill, the open-mindedness and sheer creativity that went into reaching their successful compromise. They won as individuals and as a couple.

CHAPTER FOURTEEN

LOVING SMART HAS A BRIGHT FUTURE

Relationships are living entities that change and develop, that prosper with care and disintegrate without attention. We all want romance and ever-growing intimacy in our love relationship, but the feelings are hard to come by and harder still to hang on to. Closeness itself is so complicated and modern life is so demanding that it's all too easy to lose that special feeling.

The Smartcard sort lets you get your hands on the wealth of information you need to evaluate your relationships. Armed with the Smartcards you can turn a promising relationship or even a problematic one into a union that is loving, nurturing, meaningful, and enduring. With the Smartcards you have the unique opportunity to examine your love relationships in a candid and nonjudgmental way.

Putting your cards on the table can be not only enlightening but painful when you realize you're in a dead-end or destructive relationship. Hopefully, that unhappy insight comes early enough in the relationship to save you from endless grief later on.

If putting your cards on the table has focused your awareness of a long-term failing relationship, you may need professional help before you decide what to do next. Generally speaking, psychologists, social workers, psychiatrists, addiction and abuse counselors, state counseling agencies, hospital psychiatric units, and friends who have been helped themselves are good sources of appropriate referrals if you need help.

For over eight years, my excitement has been growing with every individual and couple whom I've taught to use the Smartcards. Every time I see people put their cards on the table I marvel at the beauty and simplicity of this hands-on approach to relationship dynamics—the almost magical way the process inspires confidence and openmindedness.

I hope I've convinced you to take Loving Smart to heart. There's more than a little work involved, but the payoff in long-term satisfaction is immeasurable. Please use the Smartcards frequently as you strive to understand your love relationships. Incorporate the insights you gain from putting your cards on the table with the rest of the Loving Smart program: Follow the four-square structure, employ the protective shields, face your fears, avoid the pitfalls, and live by the five golden rules. You have the means and the method to empower your intimate love relationship to be a long-term, joyful center of excitement, challenge, and meaning in your life.

ABOUT THE AUTHORS

JEFFREY TITLE, ED.D., is a counseling psychologist who has trained psychotherapists and conducted thousands of hours of individual, group, and couples psychotherapy, as well as workshops for community and church organizations, sales personnel, and corporate executives.

ELISE TITLE, M.S.W., is a clinical social worker turned author. Her novel, *Too Many Husbands,* is in development as a major motion picture. She is also the author of numerous romance novels, mysteries, and intrigues.

JACQUELINE TITLE, M.A., holds master's degrees in clinical psychology and speech pathology. She is an educational specialist with the Richmond, California, school system.

SMART
CARDS